RONALD REAGAN'S
ROAD TO THE WHITE HOUSE

RONALD REAGAN'S ROAD TO THE WHITE HOUSE

*How Hollywood Prepared America's
40th President for the World Stage*

J. Herbert Klein

Melanie Villines

International FA Publishing
Los Angeles, California

This book is dedicated to my superior officer in the U.S. Army Air Corps 18th Air Force Base Unit during WWII: RONALD WILSON REAGAN, then a Lieutenant, later a Captain, and finally a President.

Ronald Reagan's ROAD TO THE WHITE HOUSE
Copyright © 2011 by J. Herbert Klein and Melanie Villines
ALL RIGHTS RESERVED

ISBN 10: 0-9830280-5-2
ISBN-13: 9780983028055

International FA Publishing
3183 Wilshire Blvd., Suite 196 (C38)
Los Angeles, CA 90010-1211
internationalfilmarts@ymail.com

Cover photo:
Ronald Reagan in the 1952 movie *Hong Kong*.
(Author collection)

Frontispiece:
Ronald Reagan with studio boss Jack Warner (white hat) and theater owner Sid Grauman at a movie premiere in 1937, the year the twenty-six-year-old actor started his career in Hollywood.
(Reagan Family photo collection photograph by Schuyler Crail)

Graphic design by Connie Scanlon, Bogfire. www.bogfire.com
Typeset in Minion and Calibri.

NOTE: To the best of the publisher's knowledge, photographs and other visual material in this book without a credit line are in the public domain. Errors will be corrected in subsequent editions. Please address inquiries to: internationalfilmarts@ymail.com.

TABLE OF CONTENTS

INTRODUCTION BY J. HERBERT KLEIN	6
PART I: 1937-1947	**9**
CHAPTER 1: THE SUNNY SIDE OF THE STREET	11
CHAPTER 2: THE GOLDEN STATE	23
CHAPTER 3: SECRET PASSAGE	33
CHAPTER 4: CROSSROADS	45
CHAPTER 5: BEND IN THE TRAIL	59
CHAPTER 6: THE PATH ROYAL	71
CHAPTER 7: MILITARY ORDERS	83
CHAPTER 8: FORT ROACH	95
CHAPTER 9: THROUGH THE WOODS	105
CHAPTER 10: THE WINDING ROAD	115
CHAPTER 11: THE ROAD HOME	123
PART II: IN HIS OWN WORDS – RONALD REAGAN, JOURNALIST	*140*
INTERLUDE: 1947-1949	169
PART III: 1950-1957	**173**
CHAPTER 12: THE LAST OUTPOST	175
CHAPTER 13: THE WINNING TEAM	191
CHAPTER 14: LAW AND ORDER	213
CHAPTER 15: CATTLE QUEEN OF MONTANA	227
ADDED ATTRACTION: TENNESSEE'S PARTNER	250
POST SCRIPT: HELLCATS OF THE NAVY	252
FILMS OF RONALD REAGAN	257
RONALD REAGAN'S RESIDENCES 1937-1957	258
BIBLIOGRAPHY	259
ABOUT THE AUTHORS	264
ACKNOWLEDGMENTS	266

Captain R.W. Reagan (left), my superior officer at the U.S. Army Air Corps 18th Air Force Base Unit (the First Motion Picture Unit). General Henry "Hap" Arnold, head of the U.S. Army Air Forces, initiated the unit in early 1942 to create high quality training films for enlistees serving during World War II.

(Photo: Reagan Library)

INTRODUCTION

J. HERBERT KLEIN

I met Ronald Reagan during World War II, when I served in the U.S. Air Force at Fort Roach – the colloquial name for the First Motion Picture Unit (FMPU) tasked with creating educational and training films for enlistees. At the time, 1942, he was Lieutenant, soon to be Captain, R.W. Reagan – in charge of personnel at the unit – and I was a twenty-one-year-old private.

Reagan was only thirty-one, but had already led a full life – graduating from college, working as one of the country's first sports announcers, appearing in over thirty films, and becoming a husband and father. He exuded sincerity and wholesomeness – and was like an ideal older brother, someone who'd make sure everything turned out all right.

During my time at FMPU, Reagan was always there to lend an ear or offer advice. He had a ready smile, jovial manner, and was quick with a joke or a quip. People felt good in his presence – thanks to his upbeat personality – and I was no exception.

Though our politics may have diverged at times, our values remained similar. I admired Reagan for his love of country, his faith in the American people, his big dreams and high hopes. He truly saw this nation and the people in it as a shining city on a hill.

Over the years, I followed Reagan's career, as a movie star, union leader, television personality, and finally as a politician. When his name would pop up – which, in California, was often – I'd mention that I'd served under him during WWII. Whenever I did, my companions wanted to know, "What's he really like?"

People seemed surprised when I replied, "He's just as he appears. The way he is in the movies is how he is in real life. He's everybody's best friend."

This is a book about Ronald Reagan's Hollywood years from 1937-1957. During this twenty-year period, Reagan made fifty-two movies – including classics such as *Kings Row* and *Knute Rockne: All American*. Reagan was known for his optimism – no matter what the external conditions. And in keeping with Reagan's overall outlook, for the most part this book accentuates the positive.

The intent of this book is to examine how Reagan's Hollywood career contributed to his eventual emergence on the political stage. In these pages, we'll look at Reagan's bosses, costars, directors, and friends – and explore how they influenced the man who became the fortieth president of the United States.

Much has been written about Ronald Reagan – from an abundance of aspects, time periods, viewpoints, and theories. Where does this book fit? Well, there are many works of scholarship about Ronald Reagan – written from different vantage points and worldviews. This is not one of those books. Further, we have neither a political agenda nor any axes to grind. We just want to tell a good story.

Like Ronald Reagan's Hollywood career, this book is about entertainment. It is about following along with the twenty-six-year-old hopeful who came to Hollywood during the darkest days of the Depression and set out to appear in movies that would uplift people and help them carry on. To make the reading experience vivid, we have included an abundance of photographs of Ronald Reagan at different points in his life and career, photographs of places Reagan lived and visited, as well as images of costars, friends, and family.

Much research has gone into the writing of this book, as noted in the bibliography and acknowledgments. We interviewed most living costars that worked with Ronald Reagan, made numerous visits to historical archives to examine production records, viewed every available movie, and reviewed virtually every existing book about the man known as the Great Communicator.

Part re-creation, part imagination, but all based on fact, our intention is to take the reader through the experience of what it was like to be Ronald Reagan during a twenty-year time period. For this reason, the book is written in the present tense – and it is our hope that the reader lives Reagan's experiences right along with him.

We wrote this book to celebrate the hundredth anniversary of Reagan's birth by exploring the road he traveled to become one of the most important figures in American history – and to show that he didn't end up as president despite his Hollywood career, but, instead, because of it.

PART I: 1937-1947

"In 1937…I would don my shining armour and journey to Hollywood."

RONALD REAGAN
Where's the Rest of Me?

From 1932-1937, Ronald (Dutch) Reagan works as a sports announcer at several radio stations, including WHO in Des Moines, Iowa. These are the early years of broadcast radio, and Reagan is a pioneer in the then-new field of sports announcing.

(Photo: Reagan Library)

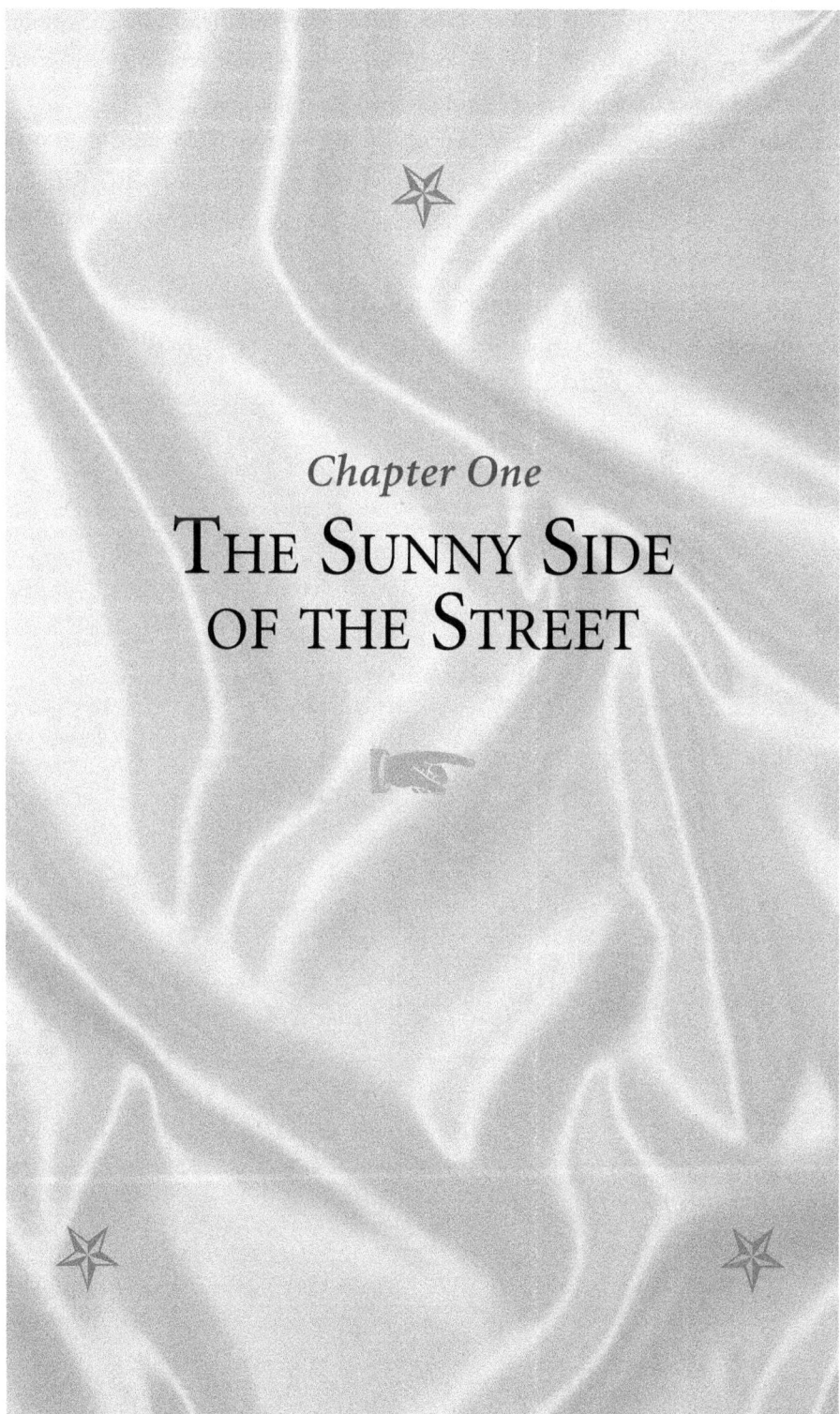

Chapter One

THE SUNNY SIDE OF THE STREET

Our story begins in Des Moines, Iowa, during May 1937. The Great Depression has been raging for nearly eight years – with no end in sight – and people across the United States are unemployed, destitute, homeless, and desperate.

But the country's woes have bypassed twenty-six-year-old Ronald Reagan – someone everyone calls Dutch, a childhood nickname he likes better than his given name. Reagan is packing up his brand-new Nash convertible and heading for Los Angeles to start a career in the movies.

And what a car! He put down six hundred of his hard-earned clams and paid for this baby in full. She's beige, she's beautiful, and her name is Sally – and she's going to sally him right to California.

A 1937 Nash Ambassador convertible like the one Ronald Reagan drives from Des Moines, Iowa, to Los Angeles, California. After signing a contract with Warner Brothers, Reagan purchases the brand-new car in tropical beige for six hundred dollars.

(Photo used by permission of private owner)

Reagan has always considered himself lucky – and believes his upbeat attitude draws good things his way. He feels humbled by his success – and knows he's among the fortunate few leaving one dream job, as a radio sports announcer, for something even better: a chance at movie stardom.

After Reagan says goodbye to his pals from the radio station, he stows his suitcase in the rumble seat, hops into the roadster, turns on the ignition, presses on the gas, and he's off.

Reagan expects only good things on the road ahead. In his unwavering optimism, he's like his mother, Nelle, who believes that things happen for a reason – and if one doesn't work out, there's something better around the next bend. Over the years, Nelle's bright outlook has been repeatedly tested, courtesy of her husband's "Irish Disease." She makes her son promise to never drink to the point of drunkenness – and he gives her his word.

From Des Moines, Reagan heads north to Ames, Iowa, where he connects to the Lincoln Highway, which traverses hundreds of small towns all the way to California.

Reagan loves touring through these dots on the map, believing that small town values are what make America great. In these hamlets – such as Dixon, Illinois, where he grew up – upstanding, hardworking people are always there to offer a helping hand and support each other through good times and bad.

As he travels down the highway, Reagan sits up high in his convertible so he can see over the windshield at the great wide-open space that is America – a place where you can dream big and have the freedom to make your dreams come true. With the wind in his hair and the sun on his face, he is the happiest man on earth – and so grateful for his many blessings.

He feels sorry that so many are out of work and so many are suffering, but believes his good fortune proves that America is still a land of opportunity.

Ever since he was old enough to remember anything, Reagan has wanted to be a movie star. The first movies he saw were cowboy pictures starring Tom Mix and William S. Hart at the Family Theater in Dixon. These were heroes, knights on horses – and Reagan wanted to be just like them, slaying the bad guys and saving the fair maidens.

From 1910-1935, Tom Mix, Hollywood's first bona fide star, makes over three hundred movies – mainly silent films. In the early 1920s, Reagan spends each Saturday at the Dixon Family Theater rooting for Mix and his horse Tony to save the day.

As the miles roll by, Reagan is more and more eager to reach his destination and begin his new career. He drives over six hundred miles the first day – reaching Cheyenne, Wyoming, by dark.

The next day in Salt Lake City, Utah, Reagan has a lead foot and a policeman on a motorcycle roars his siren and pulls over the out-of-towner – informing the speeding tourist he was doing sixty in a twenty-five-mile zone.

"Where are you going in such a hurry?" the policeman asks.

"Well, Sergeant," Reagan replies, "I'm off to Hollywood to act in pictures."

Reagan reaches in his pocket, pulls out his contract, and flashes it at the officer. The policeman eyes the piece of paper, then waves him on – another instance of Reagan's abiding good luck.

The Lincoln Highway was the 1914 brainchild of automotive magnate Carl G. Fisher (pictured here), and the first road to link the East and West Coasts - extending from New York City to San Francisco. Because it traverses hundreds of small towns, the Lincoln Highway is known as America's Main Street.

CHAPTER ONE: THE SUNNY SIDE OF THE STREET

During the 1930s there were few cars on this Wyoming stretch of the Lincoln Highway near Tollgate Rock and the Green River.

He tries to slow down, but can't manage it. He racks up another six hundred miles – finally stopping in Nephi, Utah, about a hundred miles west of Salt Lake City.

On day three, he crosses into the land of dreams – California – and rides all the way to the end of the Lincoln Highway: San Francisco. From Frisco, he heads south on Highway 1 along the Pacific Coast. It's the first time Reagan has seen the ocean – and he is so awestruck that he's afraid he might just veer off a cliff as the road winds through the mountains.

After driving through the desert in the blinding afternoon sun, by dusk he sees Los Angeles shimmering in the distance – and speeds toward this oasis. His heart is racing at the sheer romance of the journey. He's made it to his Mecca, where he will get the chance to make his dreams come true.

Finally, he is downtown checking into the Biltmore Hotel – where he stayed a few weeks earlier while covering spring training for the Chicago Cubs. During that trip, he ran into a friend from Iowa who offered to introduce him to an agent. The next thing Reagan knew, he was at Warner Brothers Studio making a screen test.

After he returned to Iowa, the agent wired Reagan that Warner Brothers had offered a seven-year contract at two hundred dollars a week. Reagan responded with a telegram that read: "Sign before they change their minds."

Now he's here, and he's on his way.

When Reagan arrives in Los Angeles at the end of May 1937, he checks into the Biltmore Hotel at 506 S. Grand Avenue.
(Photo courtesy of University of Southern California, on behalf of the USC Special Collections.)

How Hollywood Prepared Ronald Reagan for the World Stage: Reagan's Hollywood contract reinforces his belief in himself – and convinces him of the relationship between positive thinking and a positive outcome. After he enters politics, Reagan's optimism draws voters to him. During his presidency, Reagan – with his bright outlook and hopeful attitude – inspires the American people to believe in themselves again.

In 1937, Jack Warner (center), head of production at Warner Brothers Studio, offers Reagan a contract at two hundred dollars a week. Also pictured are Jack's brothers Albert (left), vice president, and Harry (right), president.

(Photo courtesy of University of Southern California, on behalf of the USC Special Collections.)

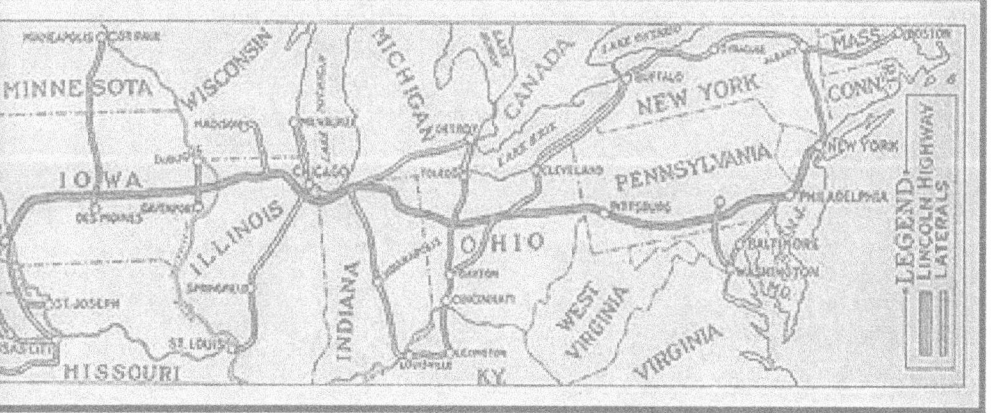

AFTER REAGAN GETS A MAKEOVER
AT WARNER BROTHERS IN 1937,
HE SAYS GOODBYE FOREVER
TO HIS MIDDLE PART.

Chapter Two
THE GOLDEN STATE

In 1937 – the year Reagan moves to California – the famous Hollywood sign reads Hollywoodland.
(The Bruce Torrence Hollywood Photograph Collection)

When Reagan arrives in Los Angeles in mid-1937, the country is experiencing hard times, but one industry is thriving – the movie business, centered in Southern California.

People want to forget their troubles and flock to picture shows to escape into a frothy comedy, uplifting musical, or exciting Western – stories where the good guys and gals win and there is always a happy ending.

Reagan looks forward to landing a role in an upbeat picture, something that will help people say goodbye to their woes for a while. Both the job and the climate suit his sunny temperament.

His agent warns that he might have to bide time until he's cast in a picture, but after less than twenty-four hours in Hollywood, Reagan gets a call to report for work the next day at Warner Brothers Studio in Burbank. He'll play the lead in *The Inside Story* – a title later changed to *Love Is on the Air* – a thriller with a three-week shooting schedule.

After a week at the Biltmore Hotel, Reagan moves to the Hollywood Plaza Hotel (seen on the left in this 1939 photo) located on Vine Street, near Hollywood Boulevard – about ten miles closer than his previous hotel to Warner Brothers Studio in Burbank.

(Courtesy of University of Southern California, on behalf of the USC Special Collections.)

Warner Brothers Studio in Burbank, California, as seen in 1928. On June 7, 1937, Reagan starts filming *Love Is on the Air* (originally titled *The Inside Story*), a drama about a crime-fighting radio announcer.

When Reagan reports for work wearing his blue trousers and white sports jacket – an outfit deemed a wardrobe "must" in *Esquire* magazine – casting director Max Arnow is appalled. He doesn't like anything about Dutch Reagan – his name, his outfit, or his haircut. Besides that, Arnow considers Reagan's head too small, his shoulders too wide, his chin too large, and his neck too short. Fortunately, Arnow likes Reagan's voice – one of the main reasons he advised Jack Warner to offer the contract.

Arnow informs Reagan that he's in a try-out period – and if Warners isn't happy with his work, the studio has the option to fire him within six months.

The changes begin with Reagan's name. Arnow tells him that Dutch will be a disaster on a billboard.

"How about Ronald?" Reagan asks.

Arnow pauses, soaking in the new name.

"I like it," he says, as if Reagan has pulled the name out of the air.

Reagan is glad Arnow likes his name, but he can't say the same. He's been Dutch as long as he can remember – and reverting to Ronald makes him feel as if he's getting baptized all over again. Well, in a way, maybe he is.

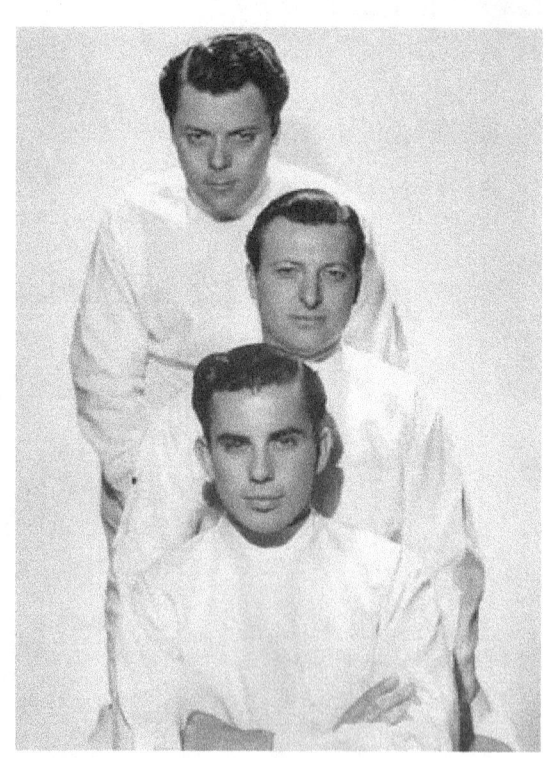

The Warner Brothers casting agent hates Reagan's hairstyle and sends him to Perc Westmore, one of several Westmore brothers who are hair and makeup artists. Considered master craftsmen, they work on many classic films and eventually earn a star on the Hollywood Walk of Fame. Pictured here are (from top): Perc, Wally, and Bud Westmore.

(Westmore family photo courtesy of Alex Westmore)

Next, Arnow orders Reagan to get his jacket altered in the wardrobe department – then sends him to the studio's hair and makeup department, headed by Perc Westmore. Reagan has been wearing his hair parted in the middle for his entire adult life, but the stylist parts it on the left, then changes it to the right.

The next day, the newly remodeled Ronald Reagan reports for work – and learns the studio has assigned him to the B unit, run by Bryan Foy. Made fast and cheap, the studios intend B movies for the second slot in double features – and use the unit to find out whether new actors have the talent and star power for A pictures.

Competitive by nature – but mainly competitive with himself and always trying to do better – Reagan dreams of getting to the A unit, heading the double bill.

Reagan reports to director Nick Grinde, and joins the rest of the cast for a read-through of the script. As he sits down for the cold reading, Reagan doesn't know what to expect. With his screen test, he'd had time to review the script in advance – and was such a quick study that he memorized his part within minutes. By the time the camera was ready to roll, Reagan knew his lines backwards and forwards and could put some real enthusiasm and emotion behind the words.

But this is different. He has never seen the script – and will have to read out loud in front of a group of professionals. When it's his turn to speak, his voice sounds as flat as the Midwestern plains, with no feeling or flavor, no oomph, no personality. He figures the director and other actors are wondering how he ended up with a swell job in a Warner Brothers picture.

Finally, and mercifully, it's all over and Grinde sends the actors home for the day. After his colleagues leave, Reagan tells the director that, considering his performance, it's understandable if he has to cancel the contract. Grinde gives Reagan a forced smile and heads out.

Reagan has visions of hopping in his convertible and heading back to Des Moines – dragging his tail behind him at thirty miles an hour.

Just then, he looks up and sees one of the studio people standing in front of him. The man introduces himself as Jo Graham, the dialogue director. Graham tells Reagan not to be too hard on himself about the read-through and offers to coach him, so he'll be ready for the next day's shoot.

Reagan is stunned at this unsolicited kindness. But he soon learns that the cast and crew are his biggest allies – and usually put themselves out to help each other.

In 1937, Reagan stars in his first picture, *Love Is on the Air,* along with June Travis. While making the movie, the duo start dating, but the relationship fizzles soon after the three-week shoot ends. "Leadingladyitis" is the word Reagan coins for an actor's tendency to fall for his female costar.

(Author collection)

The next day, Reagan reports for his first day of shooting – in a picture that seems tailor-made for him. In *Love Is on the Air*, he plays a crime-fighting radio reporter. Reagan figures he got the part because of his recent years as a real-life radio announcer – his first clue that even though Hollywood is a land of make-believe, the people in charge tend to see things in literal terms. Why else hire a radio announcer to play a radio announcer in a movie?

Graham's coaching from the previous day really pays off. Reagan hits all his marks and delivers his lines with ease. He feels on top of the world, and is hopeful he'll remain employed. But when he sees the day's rushes, his ego quickly deflates.

For the first time in his life, he sees himself from every angle – a not-so-pleasing experience. He had imagined a fictional character while enacting the part, but it's Dutch Reagan on the screen – clumsy and awkward, a buffoon going through the motions.

The shock is almost too much for Reagan's system – it seems as if he is in a dream. For a moment, he doesn't know who he is. Is he the image up on the screen or is he Ronnie Reagan from Dixon, Illinois? Is he flesh and blood, or is he celluloid?

Reagan glances at the people watching the rushes. He's pretty good at reading body language, a habit he picked up in childhood, trying to gauge the moods of his father when he'd had a few too many. Judging by Grinde's reaction, a smile and a nod, Reagan gets the impression that the director thinks his performance is fine.

Reagan wonders if he's too critical of himself. Maybe he's not that bad, after all. And maybe – just maybe – he has some talent. Whatever the case, he intends to work as hard as he can to make the most of this opportunity. He's going to arrive at work early, know his lines inside and out, and learn everything he can about the business.

In three weeks, the shoot is over, and Reagan's romance with leading lady June Travis ends soon after. It's inevitable, Reagan thinks. June is the daughter of a vice president of the Chicago White Sox, and Reagan, of course, is a rabid Cubs fan. It would have never worked out.

HOW HOLLYWOOD PREPARED RONALD REAGAN FOR THE WORLD STAGE: *Love Is on the Air* establishes the good guy type that Reagan plays in most of his movies and eventually in politics. During the shoot, he learns the value of allies, the importance of persistence, and understands that practice makes perfect. He also learns to keep the audience in mind – and try to see himself as others see him.

CHAPTER TWO: THE GOLDEN STATE

When Warner Brothers releases *Love Is on the Air* in October 1937, the movie garners favorable reviews, as does its leading man – "...poise, a voice, personality, and a face the camera loves. Reagan has all these," says Dorothy Masters in the *New York Daily News*.

(Author collection)

"I've often described those first eight pictures, or most of them, as the kind in which you could count on me rushing into the room, hat on the back of my head, grabbing a phone and yelling, 'Give me the city desk – I've got a story that will crack this town wide open!'"

RONALD REAGAN
Where's the Rest of Me?

Chapter Three
SECRET PASSAGE

At the beginning of his career, Reagan averages six movies per year. He is happy for the steady work, and feels there's only one downside — he has to provide his own wardrobe for the pictures. "…I was in a new world. For one thing, looking at my four suits — with a script in hand that told me the part required twelve wardrobe changes — and faced with a contract that stipulated male actors furnish their own wardrobe, I would wonder how the miracle of the fish and loaves was performed."

(From *Where's the Rest of Me?*) (Author collection)

Regan starts to make friends among his Hollywood colleagues – including some who live in his apartment building, the Montecito. Built on a hill, the tall building affords Reagan some beautiful views of Hollywood, especially at night. He loves living high up – and the building and its celebrity occupants make Reagan feel that he's a member of the club.

After a few weeks of living in hotels, in late June 1937 Reagan finds a permanent place to live. He moves into a classy apartment building called the Montecito at 6650 Franklin Avenue in Hollywood. Built two years earlier, the Montecito is home to many film stars, including James Cagney and Mickey Rooney. In 1985, the building – the tallest in Hollywood – is added to the National Register of Historic Places as one of the finest examples of art deco style with Mayan influence detailing.

(Photo courtesy of University of Southern California, on behalf of the USC Special Collections.)

While making *Secret Service of the Air* in 1938, Reagan starts telling people he's the Errol Flynn of B pictures. He performs all the brave exploits Flynn pulls off in A pictures, but on a decidedly bare-bones scale.

Reagan is glad he's starring as another good guy – a gallant knight who rights society's wrongs. He finds it amusing that the B unit is so low budget that some actors have to play dual roles – and end up playing a hero and a villain in the same picture! So far, Reagan has escaped this particular embarrassment.

Reagan protects Ila Rhodes from the bad guys in *Secret Service of the Air*. The two were briefly an item, until Reagan realized that he had again succumbed to leadingladyitis.

(Author collection)

A few months later, Reagan gets another chance to play heroic Secret Agent Brass Bancroft in *Code of the Secret Service*. But as they start to shoot the picture, Reagan thinks the studio should have allowed Brass Bancroft to rest in peace. To put it bluntly, the script stinks – and how can you make a good picture with a bad story?

Even so, Reagan doesn't want to be negative – hoping the editors and music people can work their magic and turn this sow's ear into a silk purse.

Producer Bryan Foy (left) and actor Ronald Reagan (center) confer with retired head of U.S. Secret Service William H. Moran, whose memoirs are the basis of the Brass Bancroft movies, including *Secret Service of the Air* (1939). For the picture, Reagan gets glowing reviews: "...a dashing hero... Bancroft is played with vigorous conviction by Ronald Reagan."

CHAPTER THREE: SECRET PASSAGE

Reagan in a dramatic scene from *Code of the Secret Service* –
a picture he hoped the studio would not release.
(Author collection)

He runs into Bryan Foy one day as the producer is rushing out of the editing room, pulling his hair.

"I give up!" Bryan says.

"On what?" Reagan asks.

"That last bomb you made," Bryan tells him.

"Hey," Reagan says, "I tried to sell those crummy lines."

"Not even God could make that dialogue work," Bryan says and rushes away.

Reagan ducks into the editing room and asks if he can sit for a while and watch the picture come together. It doesn't take long before Reagan is running from the room yanking on his hair.

He finds Bryan Foy in his office with an icepack on his head.

"Sorry to add to your headache, Brynie," Reagan says, "but you've got to bury that picture."

Bryan shakes his head. "No dice, kid. I just got off the phone with Mr. Warner himself."

"Did you tell him how bad it was?" Reagan asks.

"The studio spent over a hundred grand producing it, and they're going to release it."

Reagan and Eddie Foy, Jr., producer Bryan Foy's brother, star in *Code of the Secret Service*. Before working in Hollywood, Eddie and Bryan Foy were members of a famous family vaudeville act called The Seven Little Foys.

(Author collection)

CHAPTER THREE: SECRET PASSAGE

As head of production, Jack L. Warner (pictured in 1938) exercises total control over every aspect of moviemaking at Warner Brothers. He loves to collect Oscars and proudly displays them in his office – a sanctuary where he does not like to be disturbed. But Reagan, a relative newcomer at the studio, lays everything on the line to ask his boss for a big favor.

(Getty Images/photo by Alfred Eisenstadt)

Reagan turns and hightails it to Jack Warner's office. He's only met the boss a few times – but the head man has always been friendly and supportive. He knows it's risky just storming in to see a bigwig like Warner, but if *Code of the Secret Service* comes out, Reagan feels he'll be looking for somebody to sublease his apartment.

As he steps into Warner's waiting room, Reagan sees the boss's secretary step out. He peeks through the doorway and spots Warner sitting at his desk signing some papers. Warner looks up and notices him.

"Mr. Warner," Reagan says, "if you could just give me a minute."

Warner nods and points to a chair. Reagan takes a step inside, feeling awestruck not only by Warner and his fancy office but also by his own nerve.

He sits with his hat in his lap while Warner signs an array of documents.

"Start talking, kid," Warner says.

Reagan begins by thanking Warner for signing him a year and a half before – and says he appreciates all the swell pictures he's had a chance to appear in that have landed him good reviews.

"Your minute is up," Warner says, "and I still don't have a clue why you're here."

"Sir, the latest picture I'm in isn't really up to your high standards," Reagan says, pointing to the Oscar on Warner's desk.

Warner glances at the golden statue, then looks at Reagan.

"Either you're pretty smart," Warner says, "or you think I'm pretty dumb."

Reagan stares at Warner, not sure what to say.

"Which is it?" Warner asks.

Reagan breaks into a smile and Warner follows with a wide grin.

"I guess you can see right through me," Reagan says.

Warner stands and points toward the door. As Reagan heads out, his boss advises: "Don't worry so much, kid."

A few days later, Bryan Foy calls and tells Reagan that he has good news and bad news.

"What's the bad news?" Reagan asks.

"The studio is going to release the picture."

"So what's the good news?"

"They're not going to show it in L.A.," Bryan tells him. "None of your friends will see it."

"I have friends in Des Moines," Reagan remarks. "Lots of them."

"Tough luck," Bryan says and hangs up.

For reasons Reagan can't fathom, later in the year the studio decides to produce another Brass Bancroft adventure – *Murder in the Air*. Like all pictures in the series, this one is about protecting America from foreign invasion.

Reagan's career takes a backseat in his thoughts when the shoot begins in mid-September 1939. He is preoccupied with following what's going on in Europe. A few weeks earlier Hitler's army invaded Poland, an event that heralded the outbreak of World War II in Europe. Reagan wonders how long it will be until the United States enters the conflict. He listens to President Roosevelt's radio broadcasts, hanging onto the eloquent man's every syllable.

Still there's work to be done – even though making pictures seems trivial right now.

HITLER STARTS WAR
★ ★ ★
ITALY NEUTRAL; FRANCE AND BRITAIN MOBILIZE

A September 1939 newspaper headline announces the outbreak of WWII in Europe.

Chapter Three: Secret Passage

Casting director Arnow insists Reagan have his dark brown hair lightened for his role as Brass Bancroft, secret agent.

Before the shoot begins, Reagan gets a call from Max Arnow – telling him to head over to Perc Westmore's salon on Sunset Boulevard and have his hair lightened to auburn.

"Oh no," Reagan says.

"Oh yes," Arnow tells him. "On film, your hair comes across as jet black. Makes you look like a foreign thug."

"Would you tell Robert Taylor to lighten his hair?" Reagan asks.

"You're not Robert Taylor," Arnow says, and hangs up.

Reagan thinks the script for *Murder in the Air* is a gargantuan improvement over the previous Brass Bancroft installment. He loves the part of the story that deals with a new weapon called "The Inertia Projector," a death ray that can shoot down planes within a four-mile radius.

He has a lot of fun acting the scene where he flies a plane as his colleague prepares to use the weapon on an enemy target.

> BRASS: All right, Hayden – focus the "Inertia Projector" on 'em and let 'em have it.
>
> Brass and Hayden look down at falling quarry. They exchange grim looks as Brass offers his hand.
>
> BRASS: Congratulations, Hayden. Your invention should end all wars.

Reagan thinks it would be swell if the Allies in Europe had a weapon just like this.

HOW HOLLYWOOD PREPARED RONALD REAGAN FOR THE WORLD STAGE: The plot of *Murder in the Air* – and especially the film's unusual missile – sticks in Reagan's mind for decades, and surfaces in the late 1980s when the second-term president tries to gain support for his Strategic Defense Initiative (SDI), also called Star Wars. He envisions a weapon like the Inertia Projector that will shoot down incoming missiles from a great distance. The program creates fear within the Soviet Union – because the country can't afford to respond in kind – and is instrumental in convincing the Soviets to negotiate for nuclear arms reductions.

Theatrical poster for *Murder in the Air*, released on June 1, 1940. The movie is the third installment in the series about the exploits of Brass Bancroft.
(Courtesy doctormacro.com)

He'd rather be wearing a football jersey.

(Author collection)

Chapter Four
CROSSROADS

The year 1940 brings a big change into Reagan's life – marriage to actress Jane Wyman. But while he has settled down in his personal life, he is still looking for stability in his professional life.

Ronald Reagan and Jane Wyman meet while making *Brother Rat* (1938) – a picture set at the Virginia Military Academy – and marry on January 24, 1940.
(Photo courtesy doctormacro.com)

Soon after starting his movie career in the B unit, Reagan realizes he needs to create better material for himself. That's when he hit on the idea to develop a scenario for a picture about his idol – Notre Dame football star George Gipp. He figures his good pal Pat O'Brien would be perfect as Gipp's coach, Knute Rockne.

Reagan is so enthusiastic about the project that he talks about it to everyone he knows – and holds powwows with writers and other pros in the commissary's Green Room to pick their brains. Then one day, the boom gets lowered when Reagan opens a copy of *Variety* and reads that Warner Brothers has a Knute Rockne picture in the works.

Reagan sprints over to the office of producer Bryan Foy and asks what went wrong. Foy tells Reagan he has his own big mouth to blame – he blabbed the story to everybody who'd listen.

How can Reagan argue? It's true. But that was then. This is now. And, no matter what, Reagan has to play George Gipp – one of his childhood heroes. Foy advises him to forget it – because the producer has already tested ten actors for the part.

Reagan races off to ask – and, if need be, beg or plead – for the part from Hal B. Wallis, producer in charge of the Rockne picture. He shows up at Wallis's office and starts to make his case, but the producer cuts him off – saying Reagan looks too scrawny to play George Gipp, one of the country's all-time greatest football players.

George Gipp (1895-1920) played superb football in multiple positions – halfback, quarterback, and punter – and experts consider him one of the most versatile players of all time. To clinch the role of Gipp in *Knute Rockne: All American,* Reagan has to prove he's a real football player.

Reagan counters that he played football all through high school and college, but Wallis waves him away.

Frustrated, Reagan says, "But I'm five pounds heavier than Gipp was when he played at Notre Dame."

Wallis shakes his head and points toward the door.

To land the part of George Gipp in *Knute Rockne: All American,* Reagan shows producer Hal B. Wallis photos of himself in a football uniform.

(Reagan Library)

Outside Wallis's office, Reagan remembers something. A producer once told him that movie people don't believe anything unless they see it on film. He gets an idea – then rushes home in his convertible and searches through his trunks, finally locating photos of himself in full football regalia.

Reagan speeds back to Wallis's office and offers him the photo as if handing a holy relic to the pope. Wallis is about to shoo him out of the office, but stops, staring from the photo to Reagan and back and forth. Finally, he tells Reagan to leave the photo, and he'll get back to him the next morning.

Fifteen minutes after Reagan arrives home, the phone rings and a secretary instructs him to report for a screen test the following day.

That night, Reagan is so excited he can barely sleep. When he reaches the studio the next day, he's stunned to find Pat O'Brien in full Knute Rockne wardrobe and make-up, ready to perform during the screen test. This is highly unusual – even unheard of. Major stars don't show up on their own time to feed lines to somebody hoping for a part. What a pal, Reagan thinks.

Reagan considers The Gipper one of his all-time favorite roles. He loves everything about making *Knute Rockne: All American* – including acting with one of his best friends, Pat O'Brien (pictured at right in the role of Knute Rockne). Years later, Reagan discovers that, like Pat O'Brien, his ancestors hailed from Ballyporeen in County Tipperary, Ireland.

(Author collection)

Neil "Moon" Reagan (left) shares many things in common with his younger sibling. They both graduate from Eureka College in Illinois and both work in the entertainment business. Neil moves to California shortly after Ronald arrives in the late 1930s, and works as a director of radio programs, bit-part actor, television producer/director, and advertising executive. In more controversial matters – religion and politics – the Reagan brothers are in different camps for much of their lives. Neil is a practicing Catholic and Reagan a Protestant; Neil is a Republican, and Reagan a Democrat. While their religious affiliations remain consistent, their political persuasions eventually converge.

(Photo: Corbis Images)

The screen test is a quick scene where Rockne asks the Gipper to throw the ball, and Gipp replies, "How far?" Then Reagan, as George Gipp, throws the ball in a beautiful, highflying arc. The scene convinces Wallis that Reagan is a real football player and is right for the part.

When Reagan finally gets a script, he's pleased with the overall story – and realizes he couldn't have written a better part for himself. Screenwriter Robert Buckner developed the material with the cooperation of Rockne's widow, Bonnie. And while the story might have been sanitized, condensed, and massaged, the essence of the great Rockne is on every page.

Before the shoot begins in April 1940, Reagan and Pat O'Brien have lunch at the Brown Derby to discuss their respective roles and their relationship in the movie.

"So, Ronnie, where did your people come from?" O'Brien asks.

The question disarms Reagan. It seems off the point, but he tries his best to answer – explaining that his parents were born in Illinois, and he doesn't know much about his grandparents. All he knows is that his mother is of Scottish extraction and a Protestant, and his father is of Irish descent and a practicing Catholic.

Knute Rockne (1888-1931) was head football coach at the University of Notre Dame, near South Bend, Indiana, for twelve years. Actor Pat O'Brien – using makeup, facial prosthetics, and hairpieces – was transformed into the man sports writers called "American football's most renowned coach." Rockne's reputation stemmed from his brilliant strategy and his ability to inspire and motivate his players.

"So," O'Brien says, "at one time or another, someone on each side of your family hopped on a boat and made their way to America."

Reagan sees what O'Brien is getting at. In the movie, Knute Rockne and his family emigrate from Norway and are grateful for the freedom and opportunities they find in America – a country where anyone has a chance to grow up and become president.

Both men agree that the real star of *Knute Rockne: All American* is the good old U. S. of A. Even Notre Dame – home of Rockne's Fighting Irish – means "our lady," another way to say "mother country."

By the time the lunch is over, O'Brien and Reagan have a better idea of how they'll play their parts. They feel inspired to deliver the kind of uplifting performances the story requires.

After three years in Hollywood, Reagan is finally going to appear in an A picture. It's something to write home about, except his parents live just minutes away. When the studio picked up his six-month option in late 1937, Reagan sent for them back in Illinois. Reagan recently bought his folks a house in West Hollywood – the first that anyone in the family has ever owned. It's a small house, but Nell and Jack consider it equal to Buckingham Palace.

When Warner Brothers picks up his option in late-1937, Reagan sends for his parents, Nelle and Jack, who move to Hollywood from Dixon, Illinois.
(Photo: Reagan Library)

Reagan is relieved that most of the football scenes for *Knute Rockne* will be shot at Loyola Marymount University on the west side of Los Angeles. He won't have to spend days on a train to South Bend, Indiana – only Pat O'Brien will have to travel to Notre Dame for some campus shots.

Playing football is one thing, but playing football in the movies is something else entirely. With the camera at close range, Reagan can't kick the ball with his toe pointed, because he needs to make sure the ball misses the camera. He abandons good technique and belts the ball with his instep, sending it straight up in the air, sometimes barely missing O'Brien's head as it plops to the ground. The two actors have a good Irish chuckle over that.

Despite the fudging that occurs with playing football on screen, Reagan is still having one heck of a good time. He loves wearing a football jersey, he loves kicking the ball – but he is especially looking forward to Gipp's famous eighty-yard dash for a touchdown. On the day they've scheduled the scene, there are a lot of mixed signals, and not on the field. The director, Lloyd Bacon, and the crew can't decide what they want to shoot and tell Reagan to change from the football jersey to regular clothes, then back to the football jersey, and then back to his everyday attire. Finally, Bacon advises Reagan to take time out because the crew is going to shoot something else.

It's early in the morning and Reagan hasn't eaten breakfast. He decides it's a good time to grab a bite at the location luncheonette, where he orders a two-fisted bacon and egg sandwich, which he downs with pineapple juice and coffee.

As soon as he's stuffed himself with the greasy grub and acidic drinks, ding-dong – guess what? The assistant director instructs him to put on his football jersey – they're going to shoot Gipp's legendary mad dash for a touchdown.

The big, hot meal makes Reagan start to sweat. And he doesn't need any extra incentive – it's already ninety degrees outside. When he puts on his football uniform, he tries to pull in his stomach. It looks as if that two-fisted sandwich has left two heavy hands in his midsection.

Reagan was so looking forward to playing this scene – and he doesn't want the now-nauseating meal and hot sun to spoil the moment. He decides to put everything out of his mind except the joy he feels running for the goal and reaching it.

So he runs in the hot sun, eighty yards, with a camera on a dolly following him all the way. There are a few bobbles as the camera rolls, so the director says, "One more time, Ronnie."

Reagan puts his hand on his midsection. He feels some stabbing pains, and wonders if it could be an appendicitis attack. He is sweating even more profusely now. But this time his sweat isn't hot, it's cold. But he throws all that out of his mind. He takes the ball and he runs again, eighty yards straight toward his goal – nothing can deter him: not the opposing team, and certainly not a lead weight on his stomach and hot flames firing down from the sky.

When the take is over, Reagan bounces the ball on the ground. He made it. He did it, despite all the obstacles and discomfort. Then he hears the dreaded words: "One more time."

Best do it quickly. He grabs the ball and heads full speed down the field. Go on, Gipper, keep going, you can do it, just keep your eye on the goal line, get into that end zone, go, Gipper, go. And so he goes, but when he reaches the goal line, he keeps going – running to a wooden fence, where his breakfast makes a repeat appearance.

Reagan figures the director will want another take, but Bacon tells him the last take was spectacular. He could really believe that Gipp was on the field determined to make it over the goal line. Reagan realizes that you just never know what will impact a performance. To him, the sick stomach was an embarrassment and a nuisance. But there is a crazy logic to moviemaking. Maybe the mistake had turned into a way to motivate his performance – through no conscious effort on his part.

Reagan knows he's not much for introspection, but he can't help but wonder why the heck he ate a big meal when he knew there was a chance he might have to run eighty yards on a hot day. The ways of the thespian are strange, and no one can really figure out how to achieve a good performance. A lot of it is instinct. A lot of it is luck. And a lot of it is pure mystery. Whatever prompts the winning performance – even if it's a greasy egg sandwich – Reagan will take it. Thank you very much.

The role of George Gipp isn't a big part, but for Reagan it's a chance to display his acting ability. While Gipp appears in just one reel of the picture, it's a critical role. Gipp dies of pneumonia in a heart-wrenching deathbed scene that inspires his fellow Notre Dame players to overcome jealousy and in-fighting to push beyond their limits.

To capture the role of George Gipp in *Knute Rockne: All American*, Reagan has to prove he can throw, run, and kick.

(Photo: Reagan Library)

Reagan delivers a touchdown performance and brings to life the immortal line: "Some day when things are tough and the breaks are going against the boys, ask them to go in there and win one for the Gipper."

At a sneak preview in Pasadena, the scene unleashes a tear-fest in the audience – but Reagan remains unmoved, and can't understand why. During the shoot, he had a giant lump in his throat – and the finished product is fraught with emotion, thanks to the cinematography and the score.

Then it strikes him. How can he possibly feel sad about a character's untimely passing when he, the actor, is sitting in the audience robust and full of life? But he has no complaints – and is more than grateful for the resurrection.

The movie is a huge hit – and everybody associated with the production earns rave reviews.

Reagan realizes the Gipper won one for him. He is now a bona fide Hollywood star.

How Hollywood Prepared Reagan for the World Stage: Landing the role of George Gipp is an object lesson for Reagan in going after what he wants, no matter what the odds. For the rest of his life, people identify Reagan with The Gipper – a man who represents hope, courage, and never giving up. Reagan's Gipper qualities are in full force when he demands that Gorbachev "Tear down this wall" in 1987. At the time, few believe it is even possible to dismantle the communist bloc. Few, that is, except for the Gipper.

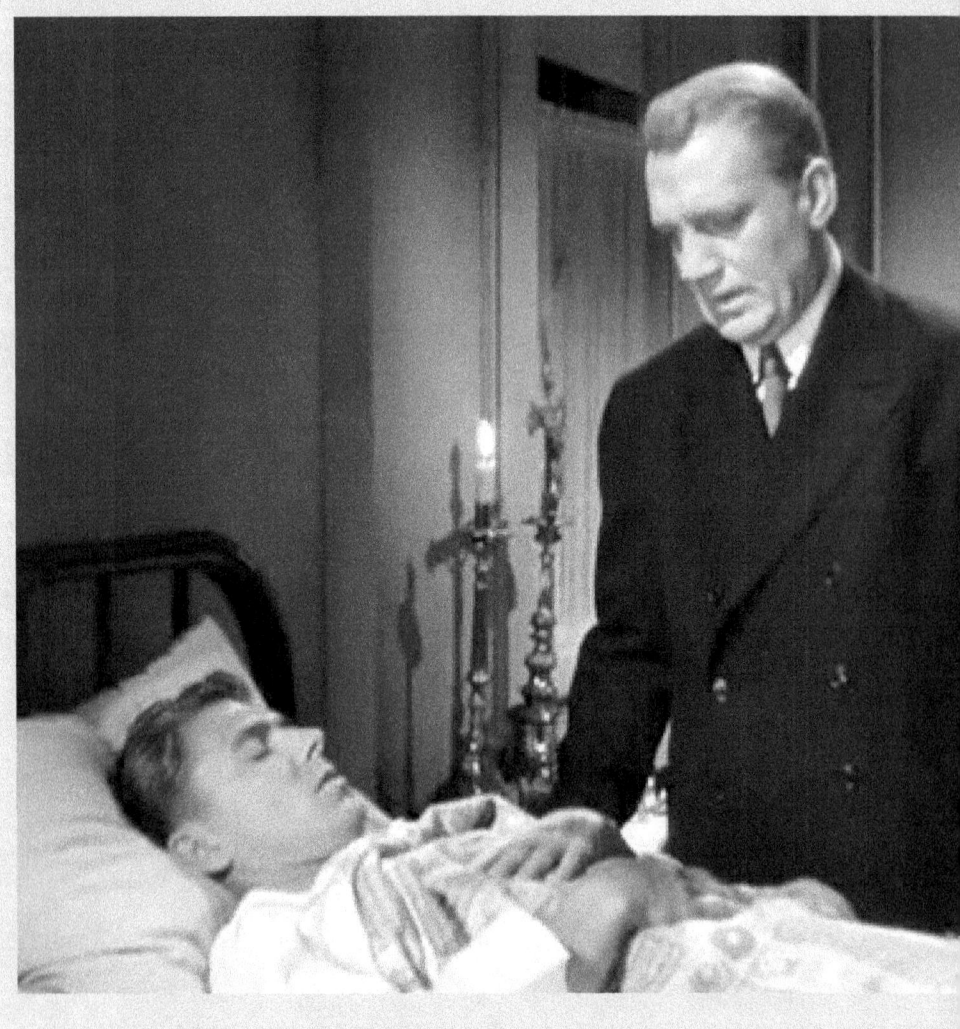

Pat O'Brien watches over Ronald Reagan as he enacts George "The Gipper" Gipp's famous deathbed scene in *Knute Rockne: All American*. (Author collection)

"For years, I've heard the question: 'How could an actor be president?' I've sometimes wondered how you could be president and not be an actor. When you've been in the profession I was in, you get accustomed to criticism in the press – true and untrue, fair and unfair – and learn to take what you read about yourself and others with a big grain of salt."

RONALD REAGAN
An American Life

Chapter Five
BEND IN THE TRAIL

AT 6'1", REAGAN IS TALL, BUT NOT TOO TALL.

(Author collection)

In 1940, Ronald Reagan, the Errol Flynn of B pictures, appears in an A picture, *Santa Fe Trail,* with Errol Flynn. The story takes place shortly before the Civil War, and follows West Point graduates — including George Armstrong Custer (Reagan) and Jeb Stuart (Flynn) — who go on to fame and glory.

(Photo courtesy of doctormacro.com)

When he gets home from the premiere of *Knute Rockne: All American,* the phone rings and a Warner Brothers secretary tells Reagan to show up for work the next morning to play a leading role in *Santa Fe Trail* — an A picture starring Errol Flynn. After three years as the Errol Flynn of B pictures, Reagan is about to work with the real thing.

The following day, Reagan reports to the studio backlot, where he finds a small army of seamstresses working like mad on the period military costumes he'll wear as George Armstrong Custer. Set in the mid-1850s, the movie follows the exploits of recent West Point graduates as they try to prevent violent abolitionist John Brown from starting a war.

The first thing Reagan notices when he walks into the wardrobe trailer is the pile of costumes with another actor's name on the inside labels. The name, Wayne Morris, is one Reagan knows well, since they worked together on *Brother Rat* and *Brother Rat and a Baby.*

When Reagan sees a custodian pick up the pile of clothes and throw them into a corner, he is shocked. It's as if the man had picked up Morris himself and dumped him on a trash heap. Reagan knows this can happen to any actor, including himself, at any time.

As he stands behind a screen trying on a costume, Reagan listens as two of the seamstresses talk. From their brief exchanges, Reagan pieces together that Morris was fired after just a few days on the picture. Reagan is familiar with Morris – as a total professional and gentleman – and wonders what his former costar could have done to get the heave-ho.

When he steps out in his Army blues, complete with gold buttons and ornate gold epaulets, a seamstress examines him, checking the fit.

Reagan wants to ask why Wayne Morris was fired, but knows better than to say anything. When it comes to gossip on a set, it's wise to look and listen rather than say a word.

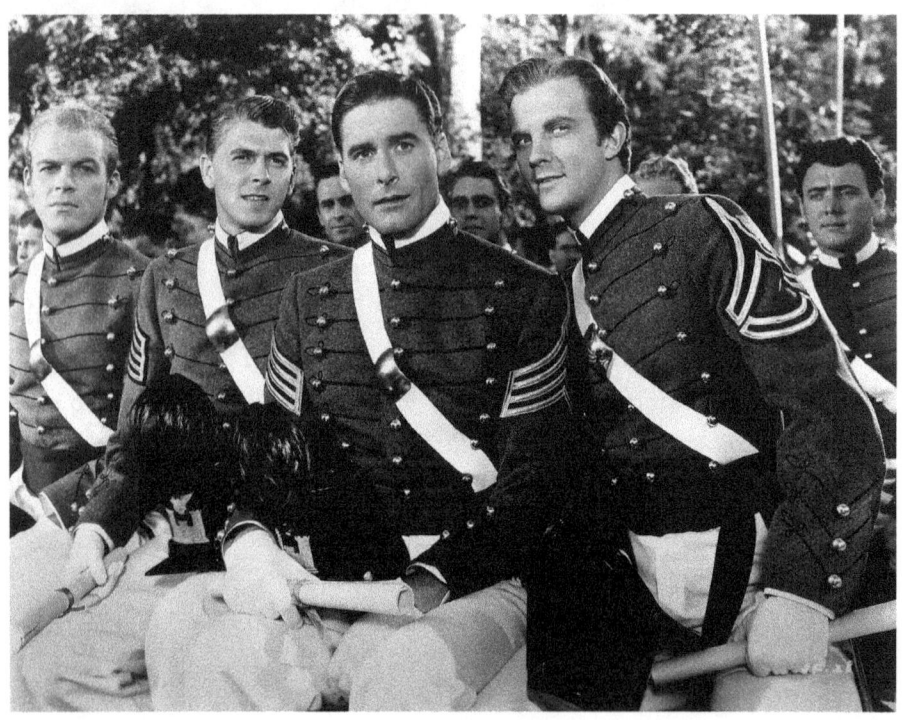

Reagan, Errol Flynn (second from right), and costars wear a variety of ornate military uniforms in *Santa Fe Trail*.

(Author collection)

For Reagan, the best thing about the picture is that it allows him to indulge in one of his great passions – horseback riding. Near his Hollywood home, he rides in Griffith Park whenever he can, which never seems often enough. Here, he'll have nearly two months on a horse – and get paid for it. He can't think of anything better.

Costumed and ready, Reagan heads off to check in with director Michael Curtiz, who has directed Errol Flynn in many pictures. Reagan has seen and enjoyed every one, especially *Captain Blood*.

As Reagan mingles with the cast and crew, it seems that everyone has an anecdote to share about Flynn, Curtiz, or both. The humor in many of the stories hinges on Curtiz's fractured English. An immigrant from Hungary, he's worked in Hollywood since the mid-1920s, but hasn't managed to learn much of the native language. After numerous run-ins with Flynn, he now refers to the star as "Earl Flint."

Michael Curtiz (1886-1962) was born in Budapest, Hungary, and enjoyed an extensive career in Europe before emigrating to the United States during the 1920s. In Hollywood, he directs over a hundred movies, including *Casablanca*, for which he wins an Oscar in 1944.

Santa Fe Trail is the second movie, after *Sergeant Murphy* (1937), where Reagan plays a cavalry officer – but it won't be the last.

(Author collection)

When Reagan introduces himself to Curtiz, the director advises him to wait in a cabin designated for the leads. On the way, he runs into a woman he admires – one of the stars of the film, the beautiful Olivia de Havilland.

De Havilland gives Reagan a warm welcome – clasping his hands and smiling – and appears genuinely happy to see him. He clicks his heels and makes a deep bow. When she tells him he has the manners of an archduke, Reagan blushes – and de Havilland says he's charming. She explains that it's refreshing to spend time with such a gentleman, since this is her seventh, and she hopes last, movie with a selfish boor by the name of Errol Flynn.

Reagan is stunned when de Havilland voices these scathing opinions about her costar. Noting that Reagan's mouth is hanging open in shock, de Havilland laughs and advises him not to worry – she's already said as much to Flynn's face.

Reagan begins to say something, but decides against it. He wonders how Flynn could have changed so much. If nothing else, the swashbuckling star has always been known for his courtesy and charm. But then the answer quickly comes to him. Flynn has the Irish Disease, just like Jack Reagan, an affliction that can make the sufferers royal pains in the posterior.

When Reagan walks into the cabin where Curtiz had instructed him to wait, there's Flynn in full costume, sitting with his feet on a chair and a cup in his hand. The close quarters reek of alcohol, so Reagan figures it isn't coffee in the cup.

As Reagan walks through the door, Flynn sets down his fortification, puts his feet on the ground, and rises to greet his costar – striding across the floor, hand extended.

"Hello, mate," Flynn says.

"Nice to see you again," Reagan tells him, shaking Flynn's hand. A few years before, they had a brief chat in the studio commissary.

Reagan wonders why Flynn is looking at the top of his head. Is his part crooked? Is dandruff showing? Does he need a trim?

A few moments later, Flynn nods and walks back to his chair, props up his feet, and quickly dozes off. Reagan takes a seat, where he remains for the most of the day.

After four days of doing nothing, Flynn snaps. He has a screaming match with Curtiz, basically saying that the director hired him under false pretenses. Flynn took the part without reading a script – and, so far, none of the actors have seen a line of dialogue.

"If this picture revolves around Jeb Stuart," Flynn says, naming his character, "then why haven't I been in one shot?"

Finally, Curtiz relents and allows Flynn to read the script, which leads to another fight with the director. As it turns out, Flynn's instinct is correct. The story spends a lot of time on John Brown, the abolitionist, a role played by character actor Raymond Massey.

When Reagan finally sees the script, he, too, is disappointed. His part is mainly in the, "Is that so, Jeb?" category. He also acts as a foil by falling in love with de Havilland's character – but it's obvious that she only has eyes for Errol, at least on screen.

Somehow the movie gets shot, inch-by-inch. The main attractions for Reagan are the horseback riding and his warm friendship with de Havilland. Several times, after a long day that has spilled into the night, Flynn announces that he's leaving.

De Havilland tries to reason with him – explaining that the cast and crew are ready to shoot, and to please stay a little longer. They've spent hours preparing for this night scene, and if they don't do it now, they'll have to work even longer the following evening. But Flynn merely turns his back and leaves.

Every time Reagan and Flynn are in a shot together, Flynn glances at Reagan's head. Reagan recalls how casting director Max Arnow told him his head was on the small side and wonders if this is why Flynn keeps eyeing his noggin.

One day, he can't take it anymore. He asks de Havilland why Flynn keeps looking at the top of his head. Before he even gets the words out of his mouth, de Havilland starts to laugh uncontrollably.

Finally, she catches her breath and manages to tell Reagan what should have been obvious. Flynn wants to make sure Reagan is still an inch shorter than he is and hasn't put lifts in his shoes.

She then proceeds to reveal the reason for Wayne Morris's quick dismissal. He had the temerity to be 6'2", the same height as Flynn. De Havilland tells Reagan that Curtiz led Flynn to believe that Morris was 6'1", but when Morris proved otherwise, Flynn gave the director an ultimatum: "Him or me."

Before Wayne Morris, Dennis Morgan had been cast in the part – but, also standing at 6'2", he soon received his walking papers.

Reagan finds this all quite sad. Here is Flynn, a magnificent specimen of a man and a fine actor who can't bear to have anyone taller than he is on screen with him.

In this still from *Santa Fe Trail*, Reagan stands behind Errol Flynn, appearing much shorter than the film's leading man – just the way Flynn wants it.

(Author collection)

With a big smile on her face, de Havilland tells Reagan that Curtiz wanted to cast John Wayne as Custer. She then remarks that, at six feet four inches, Wayne's appearance on the set would have been the end of Flynn.

During the shoot, Flynn manages to keep himself entertained with nonstop practical jokes, which aren't always so funny. During one scene, when Flynn and Reagan gallop away, Reagan's saddle falls off, sending him flying to the ground, where he takes a hard landing flat on his back. Flynn guffaws, telling Reagan next time to check that his saddle is buckled tight.

During a group scene, Flynn huddles for a moment with Curtiz, who then advises a few other actors to stand in front of Reagan. During the various takes, Reagan rakes up a mound of soil with his boot heels, so that by the time they're ready to shoot, he has a couple of inches of dirt to stand on, making him visible for all to see — and, best of all, an inch taller than Errol Flynn.

HOW HOLLYWOOD PREPARED RONALD REAGAN FOR THE WORLD STAGE: In 1980, when a reporter asks Reagan if he minds sharing the spotlight with popular Soviet leader Mikhail Gorbachev, the president replies, "I don't resent his popularity. Good Lord, I costarred with Errol Flynn."

The above still shows Reagan, Olivia de Havilland, and Errol Flynn in one of the final scenes in *Santa Fe Trail*. The picture, which opens in Santa Fe, New Mexico, on December 13, 1940, receives excellent reviews, including one in *Time* magazine, calling it, "...a brilliant and grim account of the Civil War background."

(Author collection)

> "Kings Row is the finest picture I ever appeared in and it elevated me to the degree of stardom I had dreamed of when I had arrived in Hollywood four years earlier. Bob Cummings, my costar, must have wondered in later years whether he might be a psychic of some sort; clear back then on the set of that movie, Bob had a line that he would always use on me: 'Someday,' he said, 'I'm going to vote for this fellow for president.'"
>
> RONALD REAGAN
> *An American Life*

Chapter Six
THE PATH ROYAL

AFTER FOUR YEARS IN HOLLYWOOD, REAGAN IS EXCITED TO FIND HIMSELF IN THE A-PICTURE UNIT.

(Author collection)

It's the spring of 1941, and Reagan feels strange about spending his time making movies when so many people overseas are suffering in the war. He is intensely interested in world events and manages to read several newspapers each day and listen to radio reports during shooting breaks.

At home in their Hollywood apartment, he talks Jane's ears off about the war and politics – but she's usually too busy to listen. Their daughter, Maureen, was born in early January, and Jane is a tired new mother.

When Maureen is only ten weeks old, Jane is back at work in *Bad Men of Missouri*, a western about Jesse James and the Younger brothers. Before resuming her career, Jane hired a nanny named Miss Banner, a middle-aged lady from Scotland. Grandma Nelle is also close by in West Hollywood and is always ready, willing, and able to sit with her new granddaughter.

Reagan wishes his wife would take the year off, but Jane is eager to get back to work. Things change quickly in Hollywood, and there's always another would-be starlet arriving on the bus, ready to take your place.

In May, he and Jane get away to the East Coast for a promotional tour of Reagan's film *The Bad Man*, a western with Wallace Beery in the title role.

As soon as they arrive at their hotel in Atlantic City, Nelle calls – and he and Jane worry that something may be wrong with the baby. But it's even worse news. Jack Reagan has died of a heart attack.

Reagan tells his mother they'll fly home immediately, but Nelle begs him to take a train. She fears a plane crash – and that she will have to bury husband and son on the same day. Reagan tries to reason with her, but she insists that he and Jane take the Union Pacific back to Los Angeles, a four-day journey. Reagan decides to abide by his grieving mother's wishes and endure the cramped, slow travel rather than fly back in luxury on Jack Warner's personal plane.

The funeral at St. Victor's Catholic Church in West Hollywood is attended by many of Reagan's Hollywood friends, including Pat O'Brien, with whom Jack struck up a drinking buddy friendship while Reagan was promoting *Knute Rockne: All American*. When he died, Jack was just fifty-seven years old, but had been ill with a heart condition and unable to do strenuous work for many years. Since moving to Hollywood, Jack was on the Warner Brothers payroll answering his son's fan mail – a job he enjoyed and appreciated.

After the funeral, Reagan learns about the circumstances of his father's death and feels angry and bitter. When Jack collapsed, Nelle called for an ambulance – and got mired in red tape. They lived closer to the Beverly Hills ambulance service, but, because they had a West Hollywood address, were forced to wait for a local vehicle to arrive from the other end of town. By that time, twenty minutes had passed, and Jack was dead.

When Nelle tells Reagan what happened, it reinforces his passionate dislike for bureaucracy and his belief that too many laws get in the way of common sense and rational government.

He and Jane take the next few months off to grieve Jack's death – and spend time with Nelle and Maureen. By July, both Reagan and Jane are back at work – Jane, starring in *The Body Disappears*, a romantic farce about an invisible suitor, and Reagan set to star in a picture that's a departure from anything he's ever done.

It's an A picture called *Kings Row* – a dark drama about small-town life at the turn of the twentieth century. Based on a best-selling novel of the same name, the movie tones down some of the book's more sordid aspects, while retaining much of its shock value.

Kings Row stars Robert Cummings, Ann Sheridan, and Ronald Reagan as inhabitants of a small Midwestern town.

(Author collection)

Reagan plays Drake McHugh in *Kings Row*. Like all scripts of the day, *Kings Row* requires the approval of the Production Code Administration (PCA) – a form of Hollywood self-censorship initiated in 1934 to avert federal regulations on movie content. After Jack Warner sends the PCA the screenplay for *Kings Row* in April 1941, he receives a letter from Joseph Breen that begins, "We have read with great care the final script for your proposed production titled *Kings Row*, and I regret to be compelled to advise you that the material, in our judgment, is quite definitely unacceptable under the provisions of the Production Code and cannot be approved. A picture following along the lines of this script would necessarily have to be rejected." After the studio makes changes to the script and the producers negotiate with officials at PCA, the screenplay is finally approved.

Despite his upbeat temperament and "puritan," as people kid him, ways, Reagan embraces the role of high-living Drake McHugh, who endures the wrath of the town's vicious Dr. Gordon.

Reagan believes that small town America is a place where good people live good lives and do good things. But *Kings Row,* based on the Midwestern town of Fulton, Missouri, makes him take a closer look – and consider that bad things can happen to good people anywhere and bad people exist in cities large and small.

As he prepares for his role, it occurs to Reagan that he'll deliver his big scene while flat on his back – just as he'd done in *Knute Rockne: All American*. The high drama occurs when his character wakes up and discovers his legs are missing.

The film's director, Sam Wood, encourages Reagan to explore the emotions of real-world amputees – so he visits hospitals, talks to doctors, and consults with people who have lost their legs.

Dr. Henry Gordon (Charles Coburn) disapproves of Drake McHugh and waits for a chance to teach the young reprobate a lesson.

In Kings Row, Drake McHugh experiences several reversals of fortune. The movie's dramatic impact is greatly enhanced by Erich W. Korngold's haunting score.

(Author collection)

The night before shooting the scene, Reagan can't sleep. He tosses and turns, trying to picture what it feels like to have no legs. When he arrives on the set the following day, he is exhausted, but believes this will work to his advantage and make the performance more realistic.

He sees that the customized bed has been set up, and prepares for his own private rehearsal. Already in his pajama costume, he slides into the bed and pushes his legs through the opening where they rest under the mattress.

Covered with a sheet, he gazes at his body and quickly begins to believe his legs are gone. He feels panicky and nearly hyperventilates. Overcome with anxiety, he lets his head fall back on the pillow, then again raises himself on his elbows and stares at the place where his legs should be.

Cinematographer James Wong Howe asks him to leave the area while the crew sets the lights, but Reagan pleads to remain where he is, so he can continue to explore his feelings of horror and shock at realizing his legs are gone.

ONE TAKE RONALD: With no rehearsal, but plenty of practice, Reagan delivers a tour de force performance in *Kings Row,* when he wakes up, discovers his legs are gone, and screams out, "Where's the rest of me?"

(Author collection)

Howe agrees, and Reagan lies there for at least an hour while people adjust the lights. He tries to make everything contribute to his performance, even the noise and distraction. It feels as if every nerve in his body is on the surface – raw and inflamed.

Finally, he sees director Sam Wood approach. Reagan tells Wood he doesn't want a rehearsal, to just shoot the first take. The director complies.

Like Pat O'Brien during Reagan's screen test for the Gipper, Ann Sheridan is ready to shoot the scene with him – even though she won't appear in the shot. Many actors wouldn't extend themselves this way, but Sheridan knows that her presence – as Drake McHugh's wife, Randy – will enhance Reagan's performance.

As the scene begins, Randy hears screaming. She races up the stairs to the sound of "Randy! Randy!" When she pushes through the door, Drake looks down at himself, pounds on the sheet where his legs should be and screams, "Where's the rest of me?"

Afterwards, Sam Wood says, "Print it."

Reagan feels grateful that he was able to do justice to the powerful scene. He has never felt so good or so right about his profession. He wants more parts like this – meaty roles that he can really dig into.

When the reviews are released – and he earns accolades from everyone and everywhere – Reagan feels certain that his career is finally about to take off.

"Sturdy, remarkably effective performance."
Mildred Martin, *Philadelphia Inquirer*

"Ronald Reagan as Drake McHugh tops anything he has done on the screen to date." Harrison Carroll, *Los Angeles Evening Herald*

"Reagan fulfills every promise as Drake McHugh. This is Ronnie's big chance and he makes the most of it by turning in a superior performance."
Louella Parsons, *Los Angeles Examiner*

"Ronald Reagan is excellent." Howard Barnes, *New York Herald Tribune*

HOW HOLLYWOOD PREPARED RONALD REAGAN FOR THE WORLD STAGE: Ronald Reagan's performance as Drake McHugh is a breakthrough for him as an actor. The role teaches him that to make something believable, he has to first convince himself. In politics, the same principle will hold true. To sell his ideas to others, he has to first sell himself.

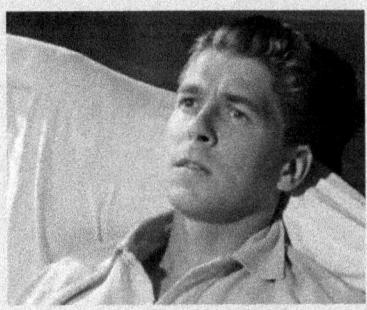

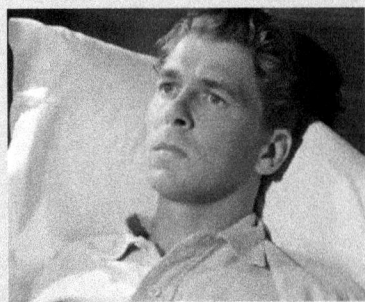

Reagan displays a range of emotions in *Kings Row* — and establishes his reputation as a serious actor.

In 1941, Reagan is on the fourth year of his seven-year contract with Warner Brothers Studio.

(Author collection)

Chapter Seven
MILITARY ORDERS

While making *Kings Row*, Reagan attends his first board meeting of the Screen Actors Guild (SAG) as an alternate for a fellow actor. After his initial appearance on August 11, 1941, Reagan becomes more and more involved in the organization.

Formed in 1933, during the past eight years SAG has done much to improve working conditions, benefits, and salaries for actors. Reagan is amused sometimes when he remembers that he didn't want to join the guild when he arrived in Hollywood – and was somewhat resentful to learn membership was mandatory. Now he sees things very differently. Without the guild, Hollywood would return to the bad old days when studios shamelessly exploited actors.

Between work, family, and SAG commitments, Reagan keeps up a hectic pace. He has little time to ride horses – and misses thinking and sorting things out while in the saddle. Reagan wishes he'd land a part in a Western – the horseback riding alone would make it worthwhile.

In 1941, Reagan and Ann Sheridan shoot *Juke Girl*, a socially conscious film from Warner Brothers about the plight of itinerant farm workers.

(Author collection)

Instead of a cowboy picture, he gets cast in a ponderous melodrama – a well-intentioned movie about itinerant farm workers. *Juke Girl* is wrapping up when the United States enters the Second World War in December 1941. The Allies have been fighting the Nazis for over two years, but Japan's bombing of Pearl Harbor finally brings the war home for Americans.

Millions of men enlist and soon many others will receive draft notices – including Reagan. When he'd reported for his Army physical a few months earlier, he'd fessed-up to fudging the eye examination when trying out for the U.S. Cavalry Reserve in Iowa, where he's served for nearly five years. He admitted to squinting his way to a passing grade – but didn't think it would matter because he was riding a horse, not firing a gun. After the Army doctor confirmed his extreme myopia, Reagan was deemed eligible for only limited service. But the war has changed everything. The nation needs recruits – there are plenty of non-combat jobs – and the government could call him for full-time duty any day.

January is full of family holidays for the Reagans – Maureen turns one on the fourth, Jane turns twenty-five on the fifth, and husband and wife celebrate their second wedding anniversary on the twenty-fourth.

Living conditions are pretty cramped, since they're living in Reagan's bachelor apartment at 1326 Londonderry in Hollywood while their new home in the hills above Sunset Boulevard is under construction.

Right after the New Year, Reagan gets a call from Hal B. Wallis, head of production at Warner Brothers, who says he's sending over two scripts and the actor can have either part.

Reagan is both flattered and amazed. This is the first time the decision is in his hands. In the past, he's just taken what the studio has given him – and never had any choice in the matter.

The next day, Reagan reads the scripts, which couldn't be more different. The first is a light comedy – boy and girl fall in love while working in an aircraft plant. The second is an action picture about a team of British Royal Air Force soldiers – volunteers from different countries – whose plane crashes in Nazi Germany.

While the role in the action picture is meatier than the one in the comedy, the latter offers him star billing, while the former relegates him to, at best, second banana. But the most troublesome consideration is that the star of the action picture is none other than Errol "I'm the Tallest" Flynn.

Reagan can't decide which script offers the best career potential, so he calls Wallis for advice. The producer tells him to take the action picture – pointing out that the script includes many key scenes for Reagan.

Reagan confides that he's had enough experience with Flynn to realize nobody's part is safe. When there's even a hint another actor could outshine him, Flynn insists that the director let him do the scene. Wallis promises they'll shoot the script as it stands. That's enough assurance for Reagan – and he signs on for the role.

Before he hangs up, Wallis mentions that Flynn specifically asked for Reagan as costar because he feels they make a good screen pair – thanks to their complementary personalities.

As Wallis relates this bit of flattery, Reagan tries to separate truth from fiction. He doubts Flynn had any high praise where he was concerned – and figures the leading man simply wants someone who won't compete with his screen sizzle, or his height for that matter.

Despite his stunning looks, charisma, and acting prowess, Errol Flynn (pictured at left in 1940) remains insecure. Reagan would later write of him (in *Where's the Rest Of Me?*): "Errol was a strange person, terribly unsure of himself and needlessly so. He was a beautiful piece of machinery, likable, with great charm, and yet convinced he lacked ability as an actor. As a result, he was conscious every minute of scenes favoring other actors."

(Author collection)

A few days later, Reagan reports to the backlot at Warner Brothers to begin shooting *Desperate Journey*. Now that the United States has entered the war, Reagan feels the premise of the picture is more than a bit rusty.

In the movie, an American, a Canadian, an Australian, a Scot, and an Englishman are on a mission for the British Royal Air Force when their plane crashes in Deutschland. Nazi soldiers capture the foreigners, but the RAF chaps manage to humiliate and foil their captors – whom the movie portrays as bumbling nincompoops. The officers then traipse across Germany, managing to sabotage the enemy in myriad and sundry ways – until finally commandeering a plane and returning to jolly olde England.

Throughout the picture, the RAF crewmembers appear lighthearted – as if everything that happens is a romp and a lark. During the shoot, Reagan has to keep reminding himself that the adversaries are based on Hitler and his minions.

In the Hollywood version, the Nazis are hard to take seriously. In fact, the movie comes across as a comedy rather than a drama – and Reagan worries that the picture trivializes the diabolical fuehrer and his evil regime. *Desperate Journey* is a far cry from news reports about the Gestapo rounding up Jews and sending them to detention camps.

From left: Alan Hale, Ronald Reagan, Errol Flynn, and Arthur Kennedy manage to escape the Nazis and wreak havoc in *Desperate Journey*.
(Photo courtesy of doctormacro.com)

From left: Reagan, Errol Flynn, and Arthur Kennedy are members of an international team of British Royal Air Force officers fighting the Nazis in *Desperate Journey*.

(Author collection)

When Reagan was reading it, the script didn't appear this silly – and he realizes it's hard to tell how dialogue will come across until the director sets the tone for the actors' performances. In this case, Raoul Walsh cares more about keeping the story moving than keeping it realistic.

And, just as Reagan had feared, Flynn tries to steal his big scene.

Raymond Massey, as Major Baumeister, head of the Nazi unit, decides to interrogate the men separately – starting with the American, Johnny Hammond, played by Reagan. Baumeister asks Hammond to tell him about his airplane – and the American launches into a spiel loaded with jargon, doubletalk, and what sounds like pig Latin. Baumeister nods, making believe he understands. Finally, Hammond knocks out the Major, then calls for his fellow crewmembers, while casually sipping a cup of coffee.

Reagan knows the scene is an audience pleaser – and so, apparently, does Flynn. On four separate occasions, Flynn interrupts the shoot, saying he's ill and needs to leave for the day. Before departing, he takes Wallis and Walsh aside and says he'll stay if they give him Reagan's scene. As Reagan watches, he knows what the Tasmanian devil is after – and hopes that producer Hal B. Wallis is a man of his word.

While director Raoul Walsh – Flynn's drinking buddy – agrees, Wallis refuses. So Flynn takes off, saying he'll return when Wallis comes to his senses.

After Flynn leaves, Reagan notices Wallis's worried expression – and wonders how long the producer can hold out against Flynn's shenanigans.

As Reagan later learns, Wallis is concerned about something else – Flynn's ability to finish the picture. Wallis is among the few – other than Jack Warner – who know Flynn is suffering from a recurrence of tuberculosis, a life-threatening lung disease exacerbated by the actor's excessive drinking and smoking. While the studio wants to keep the star's condition a secret, most of the cast and crew on *Desperate Journey* have their suspicions about Flynn – who has a wracking cough and, for a very tall man, is pencil-thin at one hundred and sixty pounds.

At last, Flynn realizes Wallis won't relent, so Reagan gets to shoot his key scene, and they finally move on with the rest of the movie.

Errol Flynn is noticeably thin while shooting *Desperate Journey* – causing colleagues to suspect serious illness.
(Author collection)

Because of Flynn's many absences, the studio adds Saturdays to the shooting schedule – something everybody resents. To make amends, Flynn brings cases of bourbon to warm up his fellow workers during the cold winter days and nights.

Reagan doesn't want to seem like an Eagle Scout, as his fellow actors call him, but knows he can't keep up with the picture's heavy drinkers, including Arthur Kennedy and Alan Hale. He thinks nobody spots him pouring his shots of booze into a cuspidor, but Kennedy reports him to the others – and they all have a good laugh at his expense.

Finally, when everybody – except Reagan – is good and drunk, they get around to shooting a scene. Reagan delivers his line, then waits for Flynn's response. In a drunken slur, Flynn turns to Reagan and says, "Why don't you go ____ yourself."

By this time, Walsh is totally inebriated. He yells, "Print" – making Reagan wonder if the director heard what Flynn said and didn't care or didn't hear it and would care in the editing room.

Between Flynn's annoying antics and the movie's inaccurate portrayal of the Nazis, Reagan kicks himself for turning down the comedy set in an aircraft plant. For Reagan, there is nothing redeeming about *Desperate Journey* – a movie that trivializes Nazi atrocities, subjects everyone to a long workweek, and makes him the butt of Flynn's ridicule.

Reagan can deal with the extended hours and the Australian star's asinine behavior, but making light of Nazism is another matter.

Since Hitler's rise to power in the early 1930s, Reagan has denounced the dictator and his regime. He has fully supported Roosevelt in his struggle against isolationists – including, most prominently, aviator Charles Lindbergh – who opposed the United States providing money, arms, and provisions to the Allies. Reagan agrees with Roosevelt on just about everything – especially that America needs to make the world safe for democracy.

How Hollywood Prepared Ronald Reagan for the World Stage: Working with outsized Hollywood personalities helps Reagan understand the value of remaining balanced, humble, modest, and self-effacing. He realizes the importance of keeping both feet on the ground so he knows where he's going and can walk a straight line to get there.

While Ronald Reagan shares lead billing with Errol Flynn in *Desperate Journey* (1942), Flynn always manages to come out on top.

(Author collection)

Reagan wears the uniform of a British RAF officer in *Desperate Journey*.

DURING WWII, FROM 1942-1945, REAGAN SERVES IN TWO BRANCHES OF THE ARMED SERVICES – THE U.S. CAVALRY RESERVE AND THE U.S. ARMY AIR CORPS.

(Photo: Reagan Library)

Chapter Eight
FORT ROACH

In March 1942, while shooting *Desperate Journey*, Reagan comes home to find a white envelope emblazoned with red letters shouting: IMMEDIATE ATTENTION ACTIVE DUTY. Inside, a missive from Uncle Sam tells him to report to the U.S. Cavalry Reserve at Fort Mason, near San Francisco, in fourteen days. Problem is, he won't finish shooting *Desperate Journey* for another four weeks.

The studio manages to get him an extension, but just barely. As it turns out, director Raoul Walsh has to finish Reagan's scenes using a 6'1" double with his back to the camera.

Jane is shooting *Footlight Serenade* – with several more pictures lined up – and when Reagan shows her the letter, she's shocked. She never imagined he would be called into service – not with his poor eyesight.

Reagan feels terrible leaving Jane with so much responsibility – a career, a fifteen-month-old, and a new home – but feels a whole lot better knowing his mother will be around to help.

After a few months serving as a liaison officer at Fort Mason, a letter arrives from General George Kenny of the U.S. Army Air Corps requesting Reagan's services at its intelligence unit in Culver City, California. The assignment will allow Reagan to help defeat the enemy with an unlikely weapon – movies.

Established a few months earlier by General Henry "Hap" Arnold, head of the U.S. Army Air Force, in collaboration with Jack Warner and screenwriter Owen Crump, the 18th Air Force Base Unit produces films that instruct, educate, inspire, and motivate enlistees.

Recently relocated from the Vitagraph Studios in Hollywood to the war-shuttered Hal Roach Studios in Culver City, the unit is less than an hour's drive from Reagan's residence. While away at Fort Mason for just a few months, it feels like years since Reagan has seen his family – and he's thrilled to be back home.

Reagan assumes a leadership role at Fort Roach – as the staff calls the base. Appointed personnel officer and adjutant, he has the formidable task of staffing up the operation – from fewer than a hundred to over a thousand.

CHAPTER EIGHT: FORT ROACH

In 1942, the U.S. Army Air Corps 18th Air Force Base Unit moves in to the vacant Hal Roach Studios in Culver City, California.

Reagan appears in and narrates many films during his years in the U.S. Army Air Corps, including *Rear Gunner* (1943), shown at right, where he plays a pilot in a twenty-minute movie shown in theaters to recruit servicemen.

In addition to enlisted men, the unit draws from a pool of top Hollywood professionals – people exempt from regular service because they're over the age cut-off of forty-two or have a deferment for physical or hardship reasons. By the time Reagan finishes adding staff, he figures the unit has a couple of hundred million dollars in talent at its disposal – paying each person just a few hundred a month.

William Holden, Alan Ladd, George Reeves, DeForest Kelley, Van Heflin, and Arthur Kennedy serve in the unit – along with other leading actors, producers, writers, art directors, special effects artists, and cinematographers.

Besides his regular duties, Reagan acts in and narrates films – starting with *Beyond the Line of Duty*, the story of a heroic bombing mission carried out a few days after the attack on Pearl Harbor by members of the B-17 Flying Fortress Unit. Reagan is elated about the assignment because he'll narrate the film in conjunction with his idol – President Franklin Delano Roosevelt.

A decade earlier, in 1932, when Roosevelt won the election as the Democratic candidate, Reagan saw the great man's positive influence close to home and throughout the country. Thanks to Roosevelt's assistance programs, Jack Reagan got his first steady job in years, distributing government-supplied foodstuffs to the jobless in Dixon, Illinois – a bastion of Republican conservatism.

Hewitt T. Wheless (pictured in the 1960s) plays himself in *Beyond the Line of Duty* (1942). Directed by Lewis Seiler and shot at Randolph Air Force Base near San Antonio, Texas, the film wins an Academy Award as best short subject. Wheless subsequently enjoys an illustrious military career, earning the Distinguished Service Cross and achieving the rank of Lt. General. He lives to see Ronald Reagan elected president in 1980 – and is proud to tell people that two presidents narrated his film.

(Photo: U.S. Air Force)

Franklin Delano Roosevelt is elected to his first term as president of the United States in 1932, during the height of the Depression. The only president elected to more than two terms, he dies while serving his fourth term in office, in April 1945, a few months before the end of WWII. Reagan is greatly influenced by Roosevelt's optimism, courage, strength, and ability to connect with an audience – and considers Roosevelt a spiritual father, mentor, and role model. Roosevelt's radio addresses inspired young Dutch Reagan to become a broadcaster, which led to his career as an actor.

As a Catholic and a liberal Democrat – and an outspoken one at that – Reagan's father had never really fit into the community. But when Jack acquired his government job, he gained status and respect. As the Depression raged, people in Dixon were more tolerant of Democrats – especially since Roosevelt was offering the first assistance anybody had seen in years.

Reagan's appreciation for Roosevelt makes him feel especially honored to narrate *Beyond the Line of Duty*. The film reenacts the heroics of pilot Hewitt T. Wheless and his crew while fighting the Japanese near the Philippines in December 1941. The government intends to release the film in theaters – to inspire the public's confidence that America can win the war.

Roosevelt's narration comes from his fireside chat radio program on April 28, 1942, where he expounded on the incredible bravery of Wheless and his crew. After Roosevelt's radio address, people want to hear more about these heroes – and the President's advisors suggest a film based on the story.

Every chance he gets, Reagan ducks into the editing room to watch the film come together. He has already recorded his narration track, and the director and editor are cutting the film to correspond with his words and Roosevelt's.

In his voice-over, Reagan cautions the pilots to remember everything they learned in flight school, and tells them to "knock the enemy on its axis."

During the editing sessions, Reagan is enraptured listening to Roosevelt's confident, inspiring voice playing over and over.

> *The bomber departed from its base, as part of a flight of five, to attack Japanese transports that were landing troops in the Philippines.*

As he listens to Roosevelt, Reagan feels Jack's spirit in the room. In many ways, Roosevelt brought meaning to Jack's life. While serving FDR's agenda, Jack kept his drinking in check. He enjoyed his role as a community leader, and tried to maintain a respectable image.

> *Eighteen attacked our one Flying Fortress. Despite this mass attack, our plane proceeded on its mission and dropped all of its bombs on six Japanese transports, which were lined up along the docks.*

Reagan senses his father right next to him – a big grin on his Irish mug – listening to Roosevelt's sonorous voice. Thanks to Roosevelt, Jack enjoyed meaningful work and job security – and responded as if he'd been waiting all his life to prove himself.

Reagan recalls some of the amazing things his father accomplished – getting jobs for men on the dole, organizing work programs, cleaning up Dixon's parks and streets, and helping build an airplane hangar. Jack showed himself to be a real leader – and in many ways acted as the de facto mayor of Dixon.

> *As it turned back on its homeward journey, a running fight between the bomber and the eighteen Japanese pursuit planes continued for seventy-five miles.*

As a child, Reagan was painfully aware of his father's alcoholism and inability to hold down a job – but tried to see past these shortcomings to the heroic Jack. His mother continually painted Jack in bright colors for her sons – and encouraged them to understand that the "Irish Disease" was a sickness, something Jack couldn't help. She reminded her two boys to appreciate Jack's rare qualities – his tolerance, courage, and fairness.

> *One engine of the bomber was shot out, one gas tank was hit, the radio was shot off, and the oxygen system was entirely destroyed. The rear-landing wheel was blown off and the two front wheels were shot flat.*

Reagan recalls that his family was among the few in Dixon that did not see *Birth of a Nation* – the D.W. Griffith film about the Ku Klux Klan that his father and mother deemed racist. During high school, when a hotel would not rent rooms to two black players on the visiting football team, Reagan brought them home – where both Jack and Nelle warmly received the boys.

Jack liked to tell the story of stopping in a hotel while working as a traveling salesman. The hotel clerk told him with pride, "You'll like our hotel, Mr. Reagan. We don't allow Jews here." Indignant, Jack replied: "Well, if you don't allow Jews, you don't allow me." He left the hotel, and headed into the subzero January night, with no place to stay except his car. A short time later, Jack suffered the first of his heart attacks – and Reagan always suspected that sleeping in freezing conditions contributed to his father's declining health.

> *With two engines gone and the plane practically out of control, the American bomber returned to its base after dark and made an emergency landing. The mission had been accomplished.*

A few months later, Reagan and Jane attend the Academy Awards ceremony, hosted by Bob Hope, at the Cocoanut Grove on March 4, 1943 – when *Beyond the Line of Duty* wins an Oscar as best short subject.

During the ceremony, as the champagne flows and the cigarettes burn, Reagan realizes that Jack – with his three-pack-a day habit and love of the grape and grain – is with them in spirit and enjoying every minute of it.

HOW HOLLYWOOD PREPARED RONALD REAGAN FOR THE WORLD STAGE: Reagan's three years at Fort Roach mark his transition into the world of government and politics. The assignment gives him experience dealing with official channels, as well as a spectrum of subjects and issues – and makes him aware of the extent of the enemy's wrongdoing. He will forever make it his mission to fight tyranny and threats to liberty.

CHAPTER EIGHT: FORT ROACH

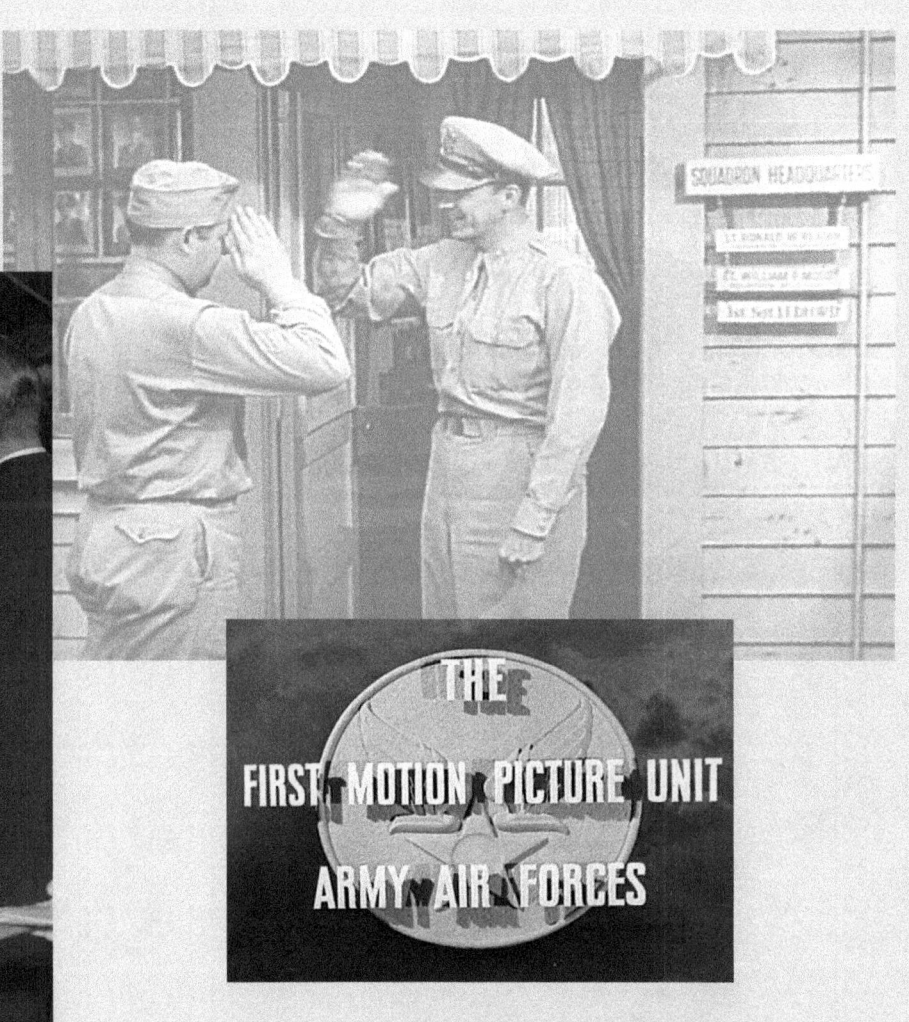

Jane Wyman and Ronald Reagan attend the premiere of *Tales of Manhattan* at Grauman's Chinese Theater in 1942. During WWII, when in public, members of the Armed Services have to appear in full uniform.

(Photo: UCLA Charles E. Young Research Library Department of Special Collections, *Los Angeles Times* Photographic Archives, Copyright © Regents of the University of California, UCLA Library)

> *"At Fort Roach, I became one of the first Americans to discover the full truth about the horrors of Nazism."*
>
> RONALD REAGAN
> *An American Life*

Chapter Nine
Through the Woods

IN *RECOGNITION OF THE JAPANESE ZERO FIGHTER* (1943), REAGAN PLAYS A FLYING ACE, LIKE THOSE HE'D PORTRAYED IN THE FEATURE FILMS *INTERNATIONAL SQUADRON* (1941) AND *DESPERATE JOURNEY* (1942).

(Photo: Reagan Library)

In March 1945, while the country is still at war, the Reagans adopt a son, Michael Edward. Maureen, now a little over four years old, has the baby brother she's been begging her parents to give her. Maureen had even tried to buy a baby brother at a local shop – taking ninety-seven cents out of her little purse and handing it to the clerk. That was when the folks realized it was time to expand the family.

On the twelfth of the following month, Reagan – like the rest of the country – is shocked when Franklin Delano Roosevelt dies of a cerebral hemorrhage. America goes into deep mourning for its beloved president, the man who'd pulled the country out of the Depression and brought people together during the war. A hero and an idol to millions, many around the world would have been surprised to learn that the Roosevelt had been confined to a wheelchair for decades.

Reagan is heartbroken at Roosevelt's untimely death at age sixty-three – just a few years older than Jack had been when he'd passed. Reagan is not embarrassed to show his grief at Fort Roach, and one of his fellow officers remarks that Captain Reagan looks as if he's lost his best friend.

In this *Los Angeles Daily News* photo from April 13, 1945, a crowd gathers to pay their respects to President Franklin Delano Roosevelt, who passed away the previous day.

(Photo: UCLA Charles E. Young Research Library Department of Special Collections, *Los Angeles Daily News* Photographic Archives, Copyright © Regents of the University of California, UCLA Library)

Franklin Delano Roosevelt (1882-1945) was paralyzed from the waist down for nearly twenty-five years — the result of his exposure to the poliovirus in 1921 — but always tried to maintain a strong image. Seen here with his dog Fala and a family friend, this is one of only two published photographs where Roosevelt appears in a wheelchair.

(Photo: American Political History)

While no one knows how long the war will last, people can sense it winding down. Combat photographers send back footage from Europe that gives new meaning to the word "raw." It is the unit's responsibility to edit the film into an information reel for officials in Washington. Reagan is present during many of these edit sessions, and what he sees makes him grow more and more political.

Reagan believes the country should have stepped in earlier to support the Allies in their fight against Hitler. The films from Europe show the devastation wreaked by the Nazis, including some particularly harrowing footage shot during close-range combat. The images are gruesome, some of the most horrible Reagan has ever seen, beyond anything he ever could have imagined.

While the big arena of the war takes precedence over everything at Ft. Roach and gives meaning to all the unit's activities, Reagan is still responsible for a myriad of mundane details. Sometimes these petty matters seemed absurd considering the seriousness of what the soldiers, pilots, and officers face in battle.

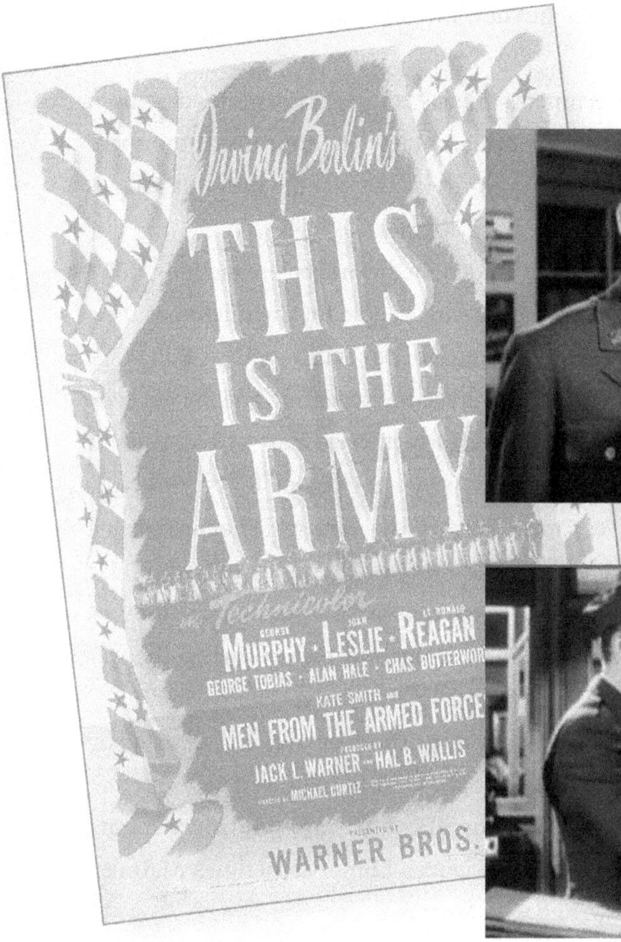

During 1943, Reagan acts in a Warner Brothers film, *This is the Army*, to raise money for Army Relief.

But somebody has to take care of the small stuff. And it is at times like these that Reagan begins to form opinions about how the government is run and decides there must be a better way.

One day, he contacts a government official for permission to destroy a warehouse stuffed with worthless paperwork and files. The unit needs the space for operations. The official response is: Yes, you may destroy the files – as long as you first make copies.

Another sore spot for Reagan is firing unqualified workers – something that's nearly impossible to carry out. Rather than reward people for the quality of their work, the government rewards people for the number of staff members that work under them. For this reason, people are discouraged from letting anyone go, even if the person is inept, incompetent, or unnecessary. In every part of government people are building empires, and the American people are paying for it.

From time to time, Reagan gives some thought to his career. He has just turned thirty-four years old, and it's been eight years since his arrival in Hollywood. He thinks about all the twenty-year-old men arriving to take their places in the movies, and wonders if there will be room for Ronald Reagan in pictures when the war ends.

Jane recently finished shooting a brilliant film, *The Lost Weekend*, directed by Billy Wilder and starring Ray Milland. This is the kind of high wattage A picture that Jane has been hoping to make. Jane is intense about her work, and often doesn't leave her performance at the door when she comes home. Sometimes Maureen runs to her dad and asks, "What's wrong with Momma?"

Nelle is practically living at the house now, helping take care of baby Michael and little Mermie, or button nose number two as Reagan likes to call her – to Jane's dismay, because she hates him calling her button nose number one.

Another thing she doesn't always appreciate is his talking politics. Reagan tries not to take it personally. He figures it's the strain of all the pictures she's making. She is doing a lot to take care of the family, even supporting Nelle. His government salary of a few hundred a month doesn't go very far when they have a luxury home, two kids, and a mother to support. Jane loves acting, so Reagan doesn't feel too guilty about her working so hard. That's the way Jane wants it.

Nelle Wilson Reagan is one the greatest influences in her son's life – for her deep faith, fairness, charitable nature, concern for others, as well as her love of dramatic art. During his childhood, Nelle gave many public readings in Dixon, Illinois, and Reagan accompanied his mother on many of these occasions.

(Photo: Reagan Library)

A few weeks after Roosevelt dies, Hitler commits suicide, and on May 8th, the Allies celebrate VE-Day – Victory in Europe. The Allied troops enter Germany to liberate the prisoners in the concentration camps, and Ft. Roach begins to receive footage documenting these events.

Reagan knows Hitler was a madman and a maniac, but nothing has prepared him for what he sees in these films. Dead bodies, people starved and then gassed, piled up like kindling. Others fester in mass graves. The living are barely alive, skin and bones, haunted, sleepwalking.

Even though it's against regulations, Reagan makes a copy of one of these films and takes it home, where he puts it in his safe. He remembers what happened after the First World War, when people started to doubt the atrocities ascribed to the enemy. He fears that someday people might begin to doubt that Hitler had done all he'd been accused of doing. If that ever happens, Reagan will have the best kind of proof – a motion picture.

Reagan in a scene from *Recognition of the Japanese Zero Fighter* (1943).

CHAPTER NINE: THROUGH THE WOODS

How Hollywood Prepared Ronald Reagan for the World Stage: Through his wartime service, Reagan gains a broad understanding of government bodies and officials – as well as the inner workings of the halls of power.

Hollywood artists at Fort Roach help win WWII – making Reagan proud to call himself an actor.

(Author collection)

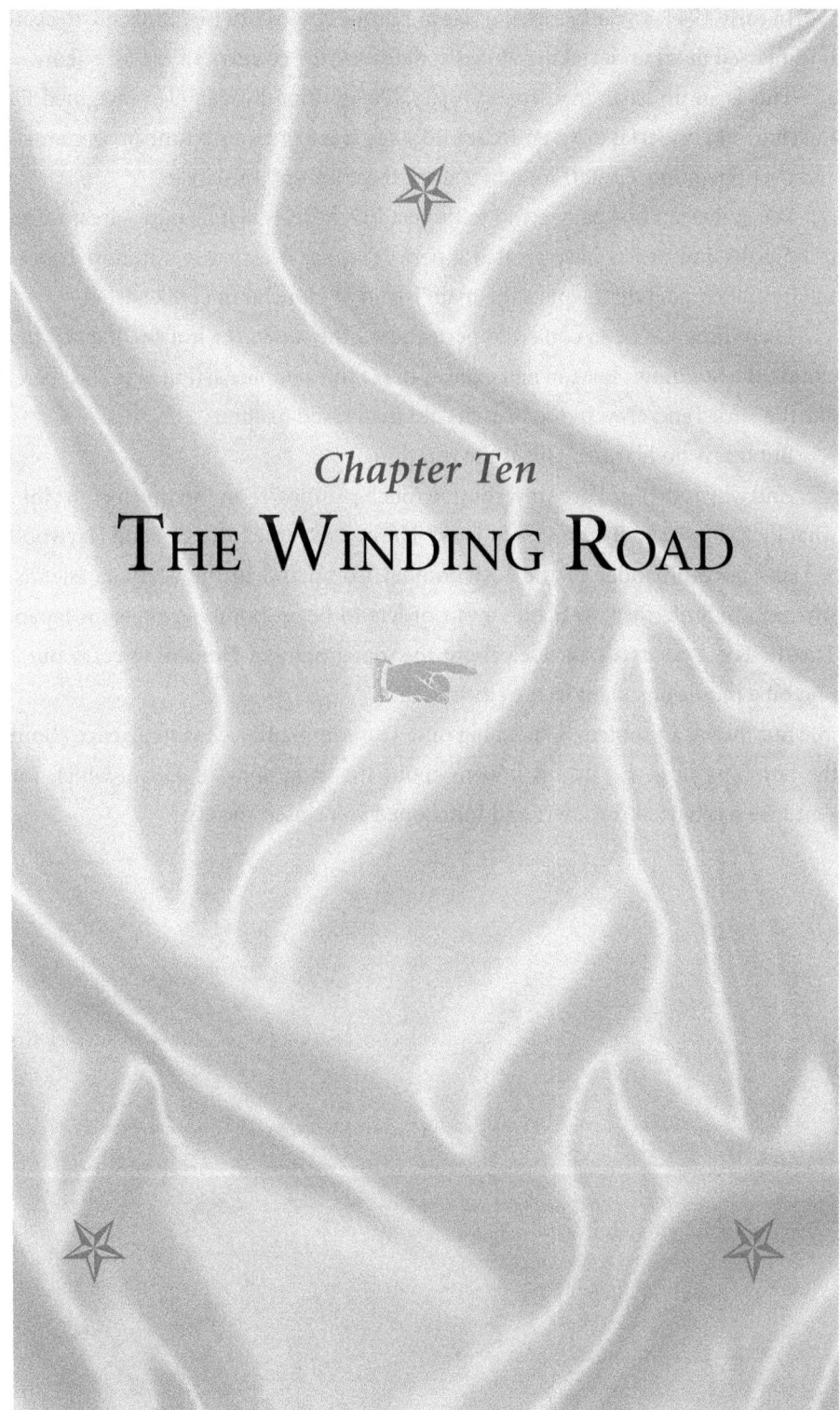

Chapter Ten

THE WINDING ROAD

In early 1944, a year before the war in Europe comes to a merciful end, Reagan is immersed in an undertaking aimed at defeating the country's Far East enemy.

This is an unusual, top-secret project, like nothing Reagan ever imagined Ft. Roach would undertake. An entire sound stage is under twenty-four-hour guard – and over one hundred staff members work there around the clock.

When Reagan first gains entry to Project 152, he feels as if he is in a dream. The technicians and artists have created a perfect replica of Japan – a hundred-foot-square scale model that depicts the main island of Honshu in lifelike detail.

Everything has been copied to perfection – the water, the houses, the sky, the clouds, the buildings. Reagan half expects to see tiny people darting here and there, like the fairies and elves in the tales his old man loved to spin.

But this is no blarney. This is the real thing.

And why is the Air Force investing so much manpower and so much effort into what looks like a small amusement park? The orders came from General Haywood S. Hansell, commander of the XXI Bomber Command in the Mariana Islands, where B-29 Superfortress planes await orders to begin bombing raids on Japan. The Air Force needs a clear idea about the topography of Honshu to carry out a raid on a munitions plant in the city of Ota.

But there's a problem – and a big one. The command lacks intelligence about the bombing targets. Little is known about the geography of Japan, which for centuries has barred outsiders and functioned as a closed society.

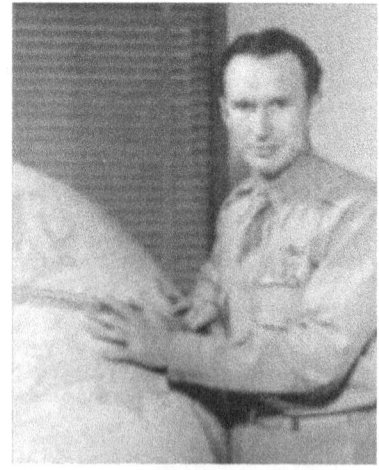

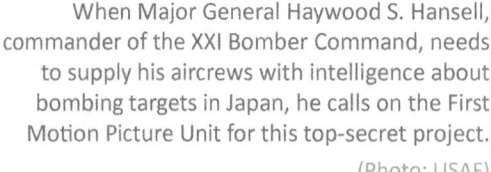

When Major General Haywood S. Hansell, commander of the XXI Bomber Command, needs to supply his aircrews with intelligence about bombing targets in Japan, he calls on the First Motion Picture Unit for this top-secret project.

(Photo: USAF)

CHAPTER TEN: THE WINDING ROAD

Paintings, such as "Mt. Fuji Seen Across a Ray" by Ando Hiroshige (1797-1858), serve as reference material for building the topographical map of Honshu, Japan's main island.

B-29 aircraft, called the Superfortress, fly scores of bombing missions over Japan. Pictured here is an actual 1945 mission with Mt. Fuji in the background.

(Photo: USAF)

The map program at the First Motion Picture Unit gets its start in the fall of 1942, when Lieutenant R.W. Reagan gives twenty-one-year-old Private J. Herbert Klein (pictured at left) the assignment to create a topographical map of California to aid military pilots flying over the state. After the war, Klein becomes a film producer, builder, and author.

(Photo: J. Herbert Klein)

General Hansell needs to prepare his aircrews for the bombing missions. He calls on the First Motion Picture Unit to create a lifelike, scale model topographical map – and hopes that the Hollywood professionals have the expertise to carry out this critical mission. Reagan has no doubt they will get the job done.

Project 152 makes Reagan proud to call himself a member of the Hollywood establishment. It's amazing what the technicians are able to accomplish with pure Yankee ingenuity. This is government intelligence in its highest form, and it's carried out not by secret agents but by Hollywood craftspeople.

Researchers pore through art books at the library, looking for paintings that might hold keys to Japan's geography. Since reference material is scarce, they also scour old newspapers, magazines, and travel brochures for clues.

Reagan is in awe of the special effects team, headed by Major Roy Seawright. The artisans work miracles with primitive materials such as plaster, spun glass, and chicken wire. These are true Hollywood geniuses – and now they are bona fide Hollywood heroes.

Little by little the island takes shape. Here in Culver City, California, in the U. S. of A., Reagan narrates to himself, we are creating a secret weapon, a model of the enemy nation, so the pilots can study it and know where they're flying and what they're supposed to bomb.

The movie crew shoots the map to simulate a pilot flying over the area from thirty thousand feet, and instructors show the footage to Army aircrews before they take off from Saipan for bombing raids. After the pilots return, they say the film made it seem as if they'd been there before.

The film includes Reagan's narration: *"Gentlemen, you are approaching the coast of Honshu on a course of three hundred degrees. You are now twenty miles off shore. To your left, if you are on course, you should be able to see a narrow inlet. To your right..."* he says, mentioning more landmarks. Finally, the payoff: *"Bombs away!"*

While Reagan regrets the loss of life and the suffering in Japan, he agrees with General Curtis LeMay, the brave commander who leads the initiative. LeMay believes you have to be in it to win it – and do what you can to end it.

It is a lesson Reagan never forgets.

Roy Seawright (1905-1991), a pioneer of motion picture special effects, starts his career with the Hal Roach Studios at age fifteen, and within a few years is head of the animation department. He is best known for making ghosts appear and disappear in *Topper Takes a Trip* (1939) and *Topper Returns* (1941). During his career, Seawright is nominated for three Oscars. He joins the FMPU as a major and works on hundreds of films while in the service. His most significant undertaking, and the one where his expertise shines, is Project 152, where he heads the team that creates a lifelike replica of Honshu, the main island of Japan.

HOW HOLLYWOOD PREPARED RONALD REAGAN FOR THE WORLD STAGE: During WWII, Reagan gains first-hand knowledge of top-secret military operations – experience that will prove invaluable when he becomes Commander in Chief.

B-29 bombers begin raids on Japan from a base on Saipan, in the Mariana Islands, on November 24, 1944. The B-29 pilots rely on visual identification of their targets – and gain needed intelligence through simulation films prepared by the First Motion Picture Unit. Toward the end of WWII, hundreds of B-29s bomb most major cities in Japan and prevent supplies from reaching the nation. The most famous B-29 is the Enola Gay, piloted by Paul Tibbets, which on August 6, 1945 drops an atomic bomb on Hiroshima – leading to the Japanese surrender and the end of WWII.

(Photo: USAF)

After Reagan returns from the service, he poses for a series of publicity photos — to get his name and image back in the public eye. Reagan hopes to regain the pre-war momentum he'd enjoyed with *Knute Rockne: All American* and *Kings Row*.

(Author collection)

Chapter Eleven
The Road Home

In the middle of July 1945, a few days after he's released from the service, Reagan hops in his car and heads for Lake Arrowhead, about sixty miles northeast of Los Angeles in the San Bernardino Mountains. During the drive in his LaSalle convertible, Reagan feels his heart, his mind, and his body expanding as if he's letting out a breath after holding it in for three years.

In 1945, Reagan drives a seven-year-old car – a 1938 Cadillac LaSalle coupe. (Author collection)

The war is over in Europe and Reagan feels confident that the conflict with Japan will end within weeks. He knows about the bombing missions and has no doubt the Japanese will surrender soon.

As he speeds down the road, Reagan glances in the rearview mirror and flashes his trademark smile. He's back on salary at Warner Brothers, earning $3,500 a week, whether he works or not.

Just this morning, Reagan talked to Jack Warner and laid it on the line. He wants to do action pictures – heroic stuff, like the tales that inspired him as a youth – stories about the cavalry, pioneers, sportsmanship, and feats of courage. He wants to ride a horse, work in the wide opens spaces, wear a badge, pack some pistols, and handle a shotgun and a rifle.

Warner promised he'd make it his personal mission to find just the kind of scripts Reagan wants.

Before he hung up, Reagan reminded Warner: "I don't want to play clichéd roles. No returning vets. I want to be a cowboy."

Reagan needs to reinvent himself. After a three-year career hiatus, he is no longer the ingénue. He wants, as he has always wanted, to play the hero.

As he drives toward the heart of the San Bernardino Mountains, he gets gooseflesh just looking at the breathtaking scenery, the stunning beauty of California. This is truly paradise on earth – and he feels so fortunate to be alive on this summer day, with the sun on his neck and the wind on his face. He says a prayer of thanks for all the blessings in his life.

After he was released from the service, Jane encouraged him to get away for a couple of weeks. She told him it would be a good way to transition back to civilian life. Besides, it would make her feel less guilty about her long shoot days.

The first thing Reagan does when he arrives at Lake Arrowhead is rent a power speedboat.

When the boatman asks how many hours he'll need it, Reagan, says: "Make it days," then corrects himself. "Make that weeks."

"You mean, you want the boat day and night?"

"That's right," Reagan responds, taking the keys.

For fourteen glorious days, Reagan does a whole lot of nothing, most of which involves the speedboat – fishing, sunning, and just kicking back and enjoying the ride.

When he returns the keys to the boatman two weeks later, Reagan looks relaxed, tanned, and happy.

"You could have bought yourself a boat," the man tells him, "for what you spent renting it."

"It was worth every cent," Reagan says, flashing his pearlies, which look shockingly white, framed by his deep tan.

Lake Arrowhead, a getaway spot for many Southern Californians, is located about an hour east of Los Angeles in the San Bernardino Mountains. Reagan stays there for two weeks after his release from the service in July 1945.
(Photo courtesy of University of Southern California, on behalf of the USC Special Collections.)

During the drive home, Reagan envisions his future like a series of billboards along the side of the road. He sees movie posters where he's sitting tall in the saddle. He's defending the weak, protecting women's honor, riding into danger, and saving the day. He can't wait to get started on this new phase of his career, and is chomping at the bit, ready to gallop into his future.

Back home, Jane is still working long hours – plus spending time with dance and vocal coaches for her role in *Night and Day*. It's been a while since she's danced or sung, and this is a big budget A picture starring Cary Grant – so she has to come off as first-rate.

To occupy himself, Reagan gets a case of hobbyitis. He wants to build something, make something with his hands, but isn't sure what. He drives to Reginald Denny's Hobby Shop in Hollywood to look around.

Film star Reginald Denny turns his hobby for building model planes into a business by opening a hobby shop at 5751 Hollywood Blvd.
(Photo courtesy of Pete Soule)

Reagan feels excited just walking through the door. The shop is stacked high with materials, tools, and plans for making model planes, ships, and trains. Just as he was smitten with the boat up at Lake Arrowhead, this time it's the ships that are calling his name.

He spends a wonderful afternoon, poring over plans, enjoying the bouquet of fresh balsa wood, and wrapping his fingers around the cool metal tools. When he's finished, the clerk rings it all up and the total comes to a whopping $105.75 – over a third of his monthly Army salary. This feels like a big indulgence, but it's just something he needs to do to get back on an even keel.

So for the next two months, when he isn't playing with the children, kissing Jane goodbye in the morning, or rubbing her tired feet at night, he's in the den where he can lay out all his materials, tools, and plans without worrying that the children will eat glue or hurt themselves on a sharp instrument.

He's building the United States Steamship America. When he picked out the model, he wasn't sure exactly why. Now, somewhere in the back of his mind, he has an idea, but it's more a feeling than a thought. He's working on the ship of state – the ideal union he envisions as America.

When the war finally ends, he imagines that people will cooperate, help each other, band together to make the country a great place – basically continue the brotherhood and unity they shared during the world conflict.

After his release from the U.S. Army Air Corps during the summer of 1945, Reagan takes a few months of R&R – building two model ships, seen here at the Reagan Library in Simi Valley, California.

(Photo: Reagan Library)

A feature describing Reagan's ship models appeared in the February 1952 edition of *Mechanix Illustrated* magazine.

As he builds the USS America, he cuts out tender bits of balsa and gently coaxes apart each piece so it doesn't break. It's a delicate operation, just as it will be a delicate operation to get the country working again, when all the service men and women return from war.

Sometimes while he's engaged in the intricate work, he daydreams about the roles he'll play. The children are still too young to appreciate what he and their mother do for a living, but by the time they're old enough to understand, he wants to appear in pictures that will make them proud – something that will cause the other kids to say with awe: "Gee, is Ronald Reagan your dad?"

Still, no movie offers are forthcoming. He figures Jack Warner has taken him seriously, because the boss hasn't tried to get him to appear in anything light and fluffy or dark and depressing. Warner is looking for a heroic role that will bring Reagan back into the public eye.

On the afternoon of August 14, 1945, Reagan is gluing together two pieces of his model ship when he hears screaming, squeals, and whoops coming from outside. Somehow, he knows right away that the war is over.

Reagan runs into the kitchen and finds Nanny Banner feeding a snack to Mermie and Michael. He scoops up his son in one arm and his daughter in the other and runs down Cordell Drive, where others on the street have the same idea. People are outside dancing and cheering. He gives each child a kiss on the cheek. Say "Hooray," he encourages them and soon Mermie is repeating "Hooray" and Michael is giggling.

After the impromptu celebration, Reagan whisks the children inside and says, "Let's have a party!" As he scoops up big bowls of ice cream, Nanny Banner protests that he'll spoil their dinner. Reagan grins and tells her, "Let's say this is dinner."

On August 14, 1945, people on Hollywood Boulevard celebrate VJ-Day. The previous week, U.S. planes dropped atomic bombs on the Japanese cities of Hiroshima and Nagasaki, an action that led to the nation's surrender. The announcement occurred at noon on August 15, 1945 in Japan – a time zone that is nearly a day ahead of the United States. President Truman shared the details of the surrender at seven p.m. eastern daylight time on August 14, 1945.

(Photo: UCLA Charles E. Young Research Library Department of Special Collections, Los Angeles *Daily News* Photographic Archives, Copyright © Regents of the University of California, UCLA Library)

A few weeks later, Reagan attends a meeting at the Screen Actors Guild and, before he knows it, he's back on the board.

In October, Jane completes *Night and Day* and jumps right into her next film, *The Yearling,* an A picture costarring Gregory Peck – an actor Reagan admires for his obvious talent, as well as the high quality of his roles. While Peck has only been in Hollywood a few years, he already boasts a best actor Oscar nomination.

From 1938-1956, the Screen Actors Guild occupies the top floor of the Hollywood Professional Building at 7046 Hollywood Blvd., as seen in this 1941 *Los Angeles Times* photo. In the fall of 1945, Reagan assumes his place on the SAG board – a position he'd relinquished three years earlier when he entered the service.

(Photo: Los Angeles Times)

Reagan had hoped Jane would or could take some time off between pictures, but she feels a sense of urgency about pursuing career opportunities. In two years, she'll turn thirty, and she's worried about her prospects drying up. She needs to establish herself as a serious dramatic actress and set the stage for a long-term career in the business.

For Reagan, still no offers from Warner Brothers. He calls Jack Warner at least once a week, and his boss always says he's working on it. While the studio has him under contract for a few more years, Reagan is starting to worry that Jack has put him on the back burner.

But in early January 1946, Warner finally calls with a project. He tells Reagan it's something he'll love.

"You get to ride a horse," Warner says.

Reagan feels his sprits lift just hearing the word. He envisions a noble steed, a six-shooter, and a shiny silver badge.

"What's it called?" Reagan asks.

"*Stallion Road*," Jack says, and Reagan can hear the grin in his boss's voice. Warner knows Reagan will love the sound of this title.

"What's it about?" Reagan says.

"It's about a vet," Warner tells him.

"I told you, Jack, I don't want to play any vets."

"It's not that kind of vet," Warner explains. "You're a horse doctor."

Reagan sighs and shakes his head. He figures this picture is set in the present, rather than his beloved pioneer days.

Warner then spells out that the picture is a love triangle. Two men are in love with the same woman.

"What's the other guy do?" Reagan says.

"He writes love stories," Jack says without a grin in his voice.

"Who gets the girl?" Reagan wants to know.

In 1946, Warner Brothers hires William Faulker to write a screenplay based on the novel *Stallion Road* by Stephen Longstreet. When the studio rejects his script, Faulkner returns to his Mississippi home. Two years later, Faulkner receives the Nobel Prize for literature. Faulkner's screenplay for *Stallion Road* is rediscovered over forty years later and published in 1989 to excellent reviews.

(Photo: Library of Congress, Prints & Photographs Division, Carl Van Vechten Collection, [reproduction number LC-USZ62-54231])

"You'll have to read the script."

"Send it over."

"The guy who wrote the book is rewriting it," Warner says. "We just fired Faulkner. Terrible job."

"I heard he's pretty good," Reagan says.

"He can't write a good line to save his life," Warner says. "I'll send you the script in a couple of weeks."

"So who else is in this epic?"

"Bogie and Bacall," Warner says, trying to sound enthusiastic.

Warner has opened up to Reagan many times about his run-ins with Bogart – an independent spirit who never wants to do what Warner tells him to do, and who is always looking for more money. Warner has had to suspend Bogart many times over the years, but has never had any kind of problem with Reagan. Warner congratulates Reagan for remaining a "good son" and always doing as he's told.

When Reagan hears the names of his fellow cast members, he feels like jumping up and shouting "hooray." Bogart is a huge star and he and Bacall are a big draw – thanks to their recent pairing in *The Big Sleep* – so their appearance will take the pressure off Reagan to carry the movie.

Reagan is delighted to learn he'll costar with Humphrey Bogart and Lauren Bacall in *Stallion Road*. The couple – shown here in *Dark Passage* (1947) marry in 1945, when Bogart is forty-five and Bacall twenty. Their marriage lasts until Bogart's death in 1957.

The love triangle in *Stallion Road* (from left): Ronald Reagan, Alexis Smith, and Zachary Scott.
(Author collection)

A few weeks later, Reagan finally gets a copy of the script, and he can't believe what he reads. Another deathbed scene! This time, from anthrax! This isn't what Reagan had in mind when he told Jack Warner he wanted to work with horses.

Well, at least he gets to ride when he's not busy dying or trying to come out the winner in the love triangle. Whatever it is, he'll take it – because he gets to work with Bogie and Bacall, stars with real screen presence and screen heat. He doesn't mind one bit basking in their reflected glory.

The picture is set to start shooting in the beautiful Sierra Madre Mountains in Santa Barbara County during March. That leaves Reagan with a couple of months to figure out what to do with himself.

He decides to start a-joining again – and gets onboard with several groups trying to make the world a better place. This leads him into a new line – public speaking. He starts going around to churches, synagogues, and civic groups talking about the country's post-war challenges and how people have to band together to realize global peace.

It feels great to stand in front of an audience, even if he's only giving a prepared speech. He realizes how much he's missed performing, and people's warm response gives him a welcome boost.

A week before *Stallion Road* starts shooting, Jack Warner calls to tell Reagan that Bogart and Bacall have backed out of the picture, but not to worry – the studio has already booked Zachary Scott and Alexis Smith for the roles.

Reagan likes his new costars well enough, but they don't have the wattage of his former cast members. He feels like fleeing as well, but he is under contract and figures it will be good for his marriage and his morale if he gets back to work – especially since he'll be spending a lot of time on a horse.

Then comes the next blow. He learns Warner Brothers has cut the budget, and the picture is now officially a B movie. The studio had planned to shoot the picture in Technicolor – and show off the grandeur of the Sierra Madres – but the slashed budget will only allow for black and white.

Reagan kicks himself for not listening to his gut. He let Warner lure him in with the promise of appearing with Bogie and Bacall. If he didn't like the picture, he should have walked away from it – just like Mr. and Mrs. Bogart did. But, as Warner said, he is the good son, and never causes problems the way Bogie or Errol Flynn do.

So now the only positive thing about the film is working on a horse. Reagan only hopes they don't make more changes and rename the film *Porcine Road* and have him wallowing in the mud delivering piglets.

He learns the picture will shoot on location for one hundred and nine days – nearly four months! He thought only epics like *Ben Hur* took that much time to shoot.

It's been years since Reagan has done any serious riding, so he looks for a professional coach to work with him on the picture. A U.S. cavalry reserve officer recommends Nino Pepitone, and Reagan and the Italian count hit it off. Reagan has never before seen anyone as expert in handling, riding, and jumping horses.

During his first visit to Pepitone's stable, Reagan meets Baby, Pepitone's beautiful black mare – and it's love at first sight. Reagan persuades the film company to rent the horse so he can ride her in the movie. He also convinces the production staff to hire Pepitone, a part-time actor, for a small role in the picture. This way, Pepitone can give him ongoing instruction during the shoot, and Reagan can do all his own riding and jumping, with no need for a double.

Nino Pepitone, a former captain in Italy's cavalry, serves as Reagan's riding coach in *Stallion Road*. After coming to Hollywood, Pepitone plays small parts in a variety of B movies. Reagan purchases his beloved mare Baby from Pepitone and the two men establish a partnership to breed thoroughbred horses.

(Photo: Private collection)

The picture turns out pretty much the way Reagan thought it would, but he does get some lasting benefits out of making the movie – the perfect horse and the ideal riding coach.

Reagan buys Baby from Pepitone and the two men decide to go into business together raising thoroughbred horses – two of the happiest decisions of Reagan's life.

HOW HOLLYWOOD PREPARED RONALD REAGAN FOR THE WORLD STAGE: Dealing with Jack Warner, Reagan gets plenty of practice in the fine art of negotiation and compromise – valuable skills for any politician.

CHAPTER ELEVEN: THE ROAD HOME

In 1947 when Reagan meets three-year-old Baby (seen here at left), he is totally smitten. He calls his reaction to the thoroughbred mare "love at first sight – leadingladyitis without reservation." Reagan rides Baby in two movies and then retires her to his ranch in Northridge and later in Malibu, where she foals many outstanding progeny, including Nancy D. She forever remains Reagan's favorite horse.

(Photo: mptvimages.com)

Part II: In His Own Words

Ronald Reagan, Journalist

Part II: In His Own Words

From June through October 1937,
Reagan writes thirteen articles for
The Des Moines Register about his
experiences as a neophyte in Hollywood.

(Author collection)

After arriving in Hollywood in 1937, Ronald Reagan writes a series of thirteen articles entitled "The Making of a Movie Star" for his hometown newspaper, *The Des Moines Register*. In the stories, Reagan displays a talent for vivid storytelling as well as a winning way with words.

From June to October 1937, Dutch Reagan lets the folks back home know how he's faring in Hollywood. Along the way, he manages to explain myriad aspects of the movie business and the role of virtually everyone who works on a picture.

These articles offer a rare glimpse into the hopes and dreams of twenty-six-year-old Ronald Reagan, and provide a front-row seat on moviemaking during the early years.

So sit back and let Ronald (Dutch) Reagan give you a personal tour of Hollywood in these excerpts from the series.

THE DES MOINES REGISTER
*July 4, 1937**

Dutch Does First Scene Over Again

Tells Interesting Details of How Movies Are Made

By Ronald (Dutch) Reagan

HOLLYWOOD, CAL.—It's a well-known fact that one swallow does not make a summer, and, similarly, one "take" in a movie studio does not make an actor.

I was a bit elated on my progress toward fame (or oblivion) at Warner Bros. Studio by the fact that somehow I had stumbled through the very first scene of "Inside Story," my first picture, apparently in an acceptable manner.

My elation, however, was short lived as I soon discovered when we did my opening scene with George E. Stone over and over again, about a dozen times. Nick Grinde, the director, had simply let me think I'd done the scene acceptably the first time to give me confidence and went back to it a little later to really "wrap it up." He was very considerate and never once broke into the middle of the scene (at first) with the lethal "Cut it."

My first experience of hearing this sharp command later made me feel like a Major Bowes' amateur must feel when he gets the gong. You get an all-gone feeling in the pit of your stomach that reminded me of the one and only time I was seasick when Lake Michigan got rough on an excursion I took from Chicago to Milwaukee.

I had thought I'd get stage fright when I first went before a camera, with such a large audience of electricians, grips, property men and assistants of various sorts, but I found that in the scene I was completely surrounded by a wall of light and I couldn't see anyone. It gave me a feeling of privacy that completely dispelled any nervousness I might have expected.

Only a regular radio microphone was actually in my first scene and that made me feel right at home because of the broadcasting I've done for so many months before being suddenly drafted into pictures. I never even noticed the movie mike for some time and I had no feeling of microphone fright such as many beginners are supposed to get.

---

* Copyright 1937, printed with permission by *The Des Moines Register.*

The movie microphone is suspended from a boom and follows you around during the action of a scene. It's always over your head and great care must be taken by the man who operates it to see that neither it nor its shadow get within range of the camera.

He operates the gadget with several handles that shoot the boom out and pull it back according to the action. It also has another little whatsit that turns the face of the mike toward the person who speaks. When there's a rapid exchange of dialogue, it wiggles back and forth in an amazing manner.

The actual mechanics of a scene may be interesting to some of my friends who never have seen pictures being made in a big studio.

The cameraman really has the last word on the set before beginning a scene, fiddling with a light here, adjusting another one there, giving instructions to the "juicers" – slang for electricians – overhead on catwalks just how much light he wants and where to put it before he gives the okay for the scene to be photographed.

The chief cameraman, by the way, seldom touches the camera itself. He tells his operating cameraman what lenses and filters to use, where to set the big camera and then devotes most of his time to the lighting. He really has to be an expert on the physics of lighting and know exactly the effect he wants.

Most of the good cameramen light entirely for "mood." That is, they know the story very thoroughly and each scene is illustrated according to the spirit to be expressed.

If it is a light, happy scene, the lighting will express it. If it is sad, the lighting will be more subdued. If there is a feeling of menace to be expressed, there will be eerie shadows on the walls.

I've heard it said that many of our famous stars, who are not so much to look at in real life, owe their glamour and apparent beauty on the screen to the expertness of their cameramen. He is one man on the set a star never wants to fight with because by a few subtle changes he could, if he wanted to, make the star look old and wrinkled and speedily unpopular with the fans.

To get on with my story – when the cameraman has said he's all ready, the assistant director calls "quiet," a cry that's always echoed by the man who operates the microphone boom.

The sound mixer presses a button that rings a bell once.

Doormen close the stage doors, warning lights automatically go on outside the stages so no one will come charging in and spoil a scene, and after a moment of absolute quiet the operating cameraman calls "Roll 'em."

Buzzers carry the signal to the sound recording room and an answering buzz registers at the camera to signify that the film in the camera has been synchronized with the sound recording film.

After a quick glance to see everyone is in place, the director calls "Action."

A moment or two of complete silence follows, the scene is begun and you're on your own.

Nothing can help you, no cues from a director as was possible in the days of silent pictures when, I understand, the director used to shout his orders to his players through a megaphone as the scene progressed. Then actors were little better than automatons moving about like puppets as the director pulled the strings.

In those days, most anyone who was fairly personable and could walk across a room without falling down could be an "actor." Somehow or other you don't hear about ribbon clerks and girls from dime stores becoming sensations overnight on the screen, since players have to read lines and really work out scenes for themselves.

Most players today at least have some background of professional training, stage, nightclubs or radio. They must have voices with personality and be able to really create an illusion with words as well as action.

After my first shot finally was acceptable to director Grinde, then came the process of breaking the scene up into close-ups and medium shots.

Most directors use what they call the "one-two-three" technique, that is first to film a scene in a long shot; then they move up closer for the medium, and finally the close-up. The same scene is done over and over, with only the camera being moved. This is so that the picture may be "cut," showing the reaction of each character to almost every line that's spoken. This makes the picture really move, and prevents dialogue scenes from getting boresome.

Of course, this was all so much Greek to me and it was some time before I discovered just what they were trying to do. On every set-up for a different angle, there is considerable delay as the lights all have to be changed, the camera moved, lenses and camera filters varied, but it was time I welcomed on my first day as it enabled me to talk things over with Grinde and Stone and get a better understanding of what I was supposed to do.

I took all morning to record the first scene on film and when luncheon was called I didn't know whether I was afoot or horseback. I tagged along to the café with Jo Graham, dialogue director, and when he asked how I liked my initiation into the movie business, I weakly replied, "If they can stand for me, I guess I can take it."

The Des Moines Register
July 11, 1937*

Dutch Pulls a Couple of Boners

Asked for a Date But June Said No!
Guess What the Director Said When Dutch Forgot the Note

By Ronald (Dutch) Reagan

HOLLYWOOD, CAL.—For a guy who got through 25 years of life before traveling west of Des Moines, east of Chicago, north of Minneapolis, south of the Ozarks, I'm certainly getting an education in this movie business.

I fully expected to be the victim of a lot of "ribbing" when I started to work before the camera. In the past, I've been sent out after left-handed monkey wrenches and other imaginary gadgets including a "curtain key" once when I ushered for a short time in a theater.

The head usher told me they couldn't start the show without the curtain key and that the stage manager had left it at the corner drug store. They ran me all over town before I finally got wise to the fact that I was the victim of practical jokers.

But nothing like that has happened to me at Warner Bros. where we're now deep in the making of "Inside Story." Instead, everyone has been helpful and friendly and I have yet to encounter the slightest trace of ill will or jealousy among my fellow workers.

I had really expected a hard battle, but things have gone so smoothly that I'm a little bit scared. It seems too good to last.

Picture making continues to amaze me. To complete a sequence, scene after scene is repeated, photographed from different angles so that the picture may

* Copyright 1937, printed with permission by *The Des Moines Register*.

be "cut" when completed, and the action kept going. In "Inside Story" cigarets are smoked profusely in one scene.

I must have puffed a dozen getting the various camera set-ups, long shots, medium shots and close-ups. And each time the cigaret had to be exactly the same length so it would match up when the cuts were made. An eagle-eyed script clerk and assistant director keep tabs on such items and make sure you don't make a mistake.

Connecting scenes are often made days apart, which accounts for the fact we sometimes see a man on the screen walk out of a door wearing one kind of a suit and appear on the other side with an entirely different one. That's due to carelessness on the script clerk's part and, believe me, when things like that are caught, he or she gets a dressing down.

In another scene, I had a pencil in my mouth. Two hours later, when the shot was repeated for a close-up, the script girl told me exactly how I had held the pencil, although I didn't have the slightest idea.

Nick Grinde, directing "Inside Story," is even-tempered and a swell egg, but when I pulled a "blooper," near the end of a long hard day, he proved he would not be at a loss for words if he ever had to skin a mule.

It was a silly stunt on my part, and I had a bawling out coming. Eddie Acuff, who plays my pal in the picture, and I had

to walk down a long hallway. The camera followed us on a little rubber-tired truck they call a "dolly."

As the scene ends, Eddie hands me a slip of paper, which I pocket, saying, "O.K. Sweetheart. I'll put it in my files." It was rather a difficult shot because of the timing. We had to walk just the right pace, with Eddie joining me at just the proper moment. We rehearsed and rehearsed and finally did it right a couple of times and then Grinde decided to shoot it.

"We'll wrap this one up and go home to dinner," he said.

Eddie and I did our walk perfectly, the lights never flickered, no one coughed or sneezed and the camera kept us right in the lens.

But when Eddie reached for the paper to hand me, his face went blank. It already was in my pocket. I'd forgotten to give it back to him after the last rehearsal. I felt like a sap, but there was nothing to do but go through the whole business again.

Any movie scene not actually made on the studio lot is called a "location." It may be in Alaska, in Africa, or just a block away, but it's "location." My first one was in "Thirty Acres," a site about a mile from Warners' Burbank, Cal., studio, which is frequently used.

We were to make an outdoor scene where a kids' bicycle track and grandstand had been built and when I arrived at 8 o'clock, I found hundreds of children, seated at regular school benches with dozens of teachers giving them their classroom lessons.

All children of school age working in pictures must spend so many hours at their regular studies while engaged at the studios. The teachers are supplied by the Los Angeles school board, although the studios pay them.

Our regular crew was on the job, but instead of setting up arc lights as they do on stages, they were adjusting big reflectors with silver and copper paper on their surfaces to focus the sunlight. Everything needed had been hauled to location in studio trucks and unloading them reminded me of a circus getting ready for a performance.

We put in a long, hot day before we completed the kids' bike race sequence, stopping for an hour at noon for lunch. Box lunches were sent from the studio and it was my first experience with this famous Hollywood institution.

Each box, I discovered, contained half a fried chicken, a jelly and cheese sandwich, an apple or banana, a piece of cake, pickles, a hard boiled egg, and a candy bar.

There were also half-pint bottles of milk, kept cool with dry ice – more than enough for one apiece – and big cans of hot coffee for adults. It was just like a picnic at Grand View or Greenwood.

Actors, directors, everyone got the same things. There's no preference shown when a studio feeds a location company. "Extras" like locations of this sort because it means they don't have to spend their hard earned money for eats.

Speaking of children, I was interested to learn they are not allowed to work at night in pictures. I discovered this when I saw a tree-lined street setting at the studio being covered with huge black canvas curtains stretched across the building tops and curtaining off the ends of the street.

Director Grinde explained he was preparing for a night scene in which kids would be used, so they had to make a forenoon look like midnight. The black backgrounds and dark filters in the camera will do the trick.

I'm learning new things every day but there's one thing I don't think I'll ever get accustomed to, and that is powdering my nose while the whole company looks on.

Working under the hot lights in make-up is guaranteed to bring perspiration to your face but it's always a shock to me to have the cameraman yell, "Take the shine off your nose," and have a make-up man dash up and slap my pan with a powder puff.

I've rambled all over the place in this installment and might as well stray a little farther to tell how I spoiled a scene the other day. It's the next to the last one in the picture where I "get the gal."

I whisper into June Travis' ear, she smiles and whispers in mine. To make it more realistic, director Grinde told us to say something to each other, although it wouldn't be picked up on the soundtrack.

I took this chance to ask June to dinner with me. She whispered her answer, which I didn't catch, and before I thought, I said out loud, "I didn't hear you," ruining the "take" and earning a horse laugh from the crew, which was quick to catch onto my strategy. So we had to do it again.

I whispered my question over; this time, heard her reply.

Her answer was "No."

THE DES MOINES REGISTER
July 25, 1937

Dutch Sees the Sights of Movie Lot

Tries for Date, but Misses

By Ronald (Dutch) Reagan

HOLLYWOOD, CAL.—Everyone's heard about the sailor renting a boat and going for a row on the park lake on his day off.

Well, that's me all over. With "Inside Story" finished and delivered to the cutting room at 7 o'clock of a Monday evening, I at last found myself facing the prospect of a lay-off and a little leisure to take Hollywood apart to see what makes it tick.

But Tuesday – with nothing in the world to do but loaf – I suddenly found myself at the Warner Brothers lot wandering around looking for something to do.

I strolled into the Green Room at lunchtime looking for some of my new pals with whom I'd been working. But they're old hands at the game, and disappear as soon as a picture is finished.

I'd no more than finished my sandwich and iced tea when my candid camera friend corralled me and broke the news that we were down for a tour of the lot.

Some day, if and when I'm a successful star, maybe I'll tell this fiend in human form to go climb an anthill or something. But right now, I smile and do what anyone tells me. I'd made up my mind to go for a horseback ride, too, but that was out.

I'm glad, though, that I went along with him to that section of the studio known as the "back lot."

There are acres and acres of ground, nearly a hundred of them, surrounding the studio proper where the sound stages are ranged in symmetrical rows.

These big box-like buildings are oblong in shape, built without windows and all large enough to serve as airplane hangars. There are 19 in all, each averaging about 40 feet in height and 750 feet long by 135 feet wide.

There's one big baby with an inside clearance of 70 feet, the highest sound stage in Hollywood, while another one is

* Copyright 1937, printed with permission by *The Des Moines Register*.

435 feet long by 200 feet wide. This stage was used for the Westminster Abbey set where the coronation scene for "Prince and the Pauper" was filmed.

But to get back to my tour. We started at the inner gate where an official pass is needed to get past Albert S. LeDuc, popularly known as "Duke." He's the most popular cop on the lot and kind and friendly, except when he thinks someone's trying to put something over on him.

We walked to the extreme southern end of the lot, where the Crafts building houses the mechanical and carpenter departments. There, all the sets are built and hauled piecemeal to the stages.

I marveled at the machinery and the skill of the hundreds of workmen who turn out in intricate detail everything from a simple cottage to a seaworthy submarine.

While there, I was snapped in the torpedo room of the sub, which, I understand, has been varied enough in design to confuse possible spies who will see the picture and try to steal Uncle Sam's war secrets.

Back of the building is a gigantic incinerator where discarded sets go up in smoke.

Several blocks eastward we passed the scene docks where every conceivable section, door, window, balustrade, stairway, etc., and parts of former sets are standing. They sometimes are adaptable for other sets when they're needed in a big hurry, which is why they are saved.

We found a miniature skyscraper and a model of an apartment house and climbed up the side to take a look. These

models are complete in every detail, even with little windows that can be moved up and down.

Another model we saw was that of a Chicago newspaper building.

The publicity department has a favorite story about making a tour of the world in 20 minutes by visiting the various streets and sections on the back lot.

The tour of the world part of it is okay but I'm doubtful about the 20 minutes unless you ride. When you hotfoot it, like we did, it takes a lot longer than that.

It really is an amazing sight, though. You walk though typical village streets, which might be any town in Iowa or elsewhere in the Middle West with attractive homes, lawns, trees, and fences. Then you turn a corner and are on an old frontier street.

On this street is a "haunted" house, which I was persuaded to visit and holler "boo" through the front door. If it sounds a bit balmy, don't worry. That's the way you get when you've been in pictures for a while.

My dogs were really barking by this time as the streets are merely dirt roads up and down grade and not level concrete like the regular studio avenues. Just when I was beginning to complain, we wandered onto the cobblestone streets of provincial France.

They told me to climb up a ladder and look over the set and I'd see China. Sure enough, on one side was a Chinese setting and looking the other way I saw the big galleon used in "Captain Blood."

Around the corner from France, I walked through a typical English village. One minute later, I spotted an arrow sign which said "Hudson Tunnel" and I knew I was on Canal Street, New York, New York.

Not far from there was a section of the Grand Canal of Venice built in a huge tank about a hundred yards across from the Italian city of Livorno from "Anthony Adverse" adjoining.

There was a section of Vienna, too. Then on our homeward walk we paraded down Fifth Avenue's shopping district and turned a corner, which brought us to a row of brownstone fronts of New York's tenderloin.

Having completed my studio tour, I stopped by the post office on the lot to see if I had a letter. To my amazement, I found a stack of "fan letters" written by people who've read some of my articles in *The Sunday Register*. So maybe I'm an actor, after all.

They tell me that no one's an actor until he's received his first fan letter. True, none of my correspondents has seen me act and won't until "Inside Story" is released but it's swell of them, anyway, to write to wish me success.

It's grand, too, to hear from the folks back home and it cheers me up a lot when I'm feeling a little bit homesick for the beautiful, green, rolling hills and the tall cornfields.

THE DES MOINES REGISTER
August 1, 1937*

Bosses Changed Their Minds So Dutch Makes Part of His First Picture All Over Again

By Ronald (Dutch) Reagan

HOLLYWOOD, CAL. — There's nothing like a good word from home to cheer a fellow up when he's beginning to wonder if it's worthwhile to give up all his friends and start fresh in a field entirely different from anything he has ever known.

So you may imagine how elated and happy I am to have a whole bundle of mail from friends and well wishers, especially from Iowa. They came along just at a time I was feeling a bit low, having finished my first picture, "Love Is On the Air," for Warner Bros. and was trying vainly to peer into the future and see what it held in store.

The picture, by the way, no longer is "Inside Story," but has a brand new title which the studio chiefs think – and I do, too – is much stronger. It is "Love Is On the Air," which has a swing and a lilt the other title lacked.

I've see a lot of the rushes and piecemeal they look pretty good, even to me who, not so many weeks ago, thought a "rush" had something to do with a college fraternity or trying to get aboard an L train in Chicago, Ill., during busy hours.

I guess nearly everyone who is in pictures or is permitted to shout over the radio has a few fans – otherwise they wouldn't be there. But I don't think I'll ever get over the thrill of hearing from people I've never seen praising my work and wishing me well.

* Copyright 1937, printed with permission by *The Des Moines Register*.

Most of my "fan" mail so far, of course, is from people who heard my sports broadcast over radio station WHO in Des Moines and for some reason or other decided I might do. I have several notes, however, from New York, N.Y., Milwaukee, Wis., San Diego, Cal., and places like that from people who have read some blurbs the publicity department has sent out about me.

If, when my pictures are shown on the screen, people really do like me I can see already that I'm apt to get writer's cramp. Errol Flynn, Kay Francis, Dick Powell, Joan Blondell, and big shots like that get thousands of letters a week, and it's a problem for them to handle.

Pat O'Brien, while he also gets a wagonload of letters every day, tells me he reads every one and answers those that call for an answer.

Most letters ask for pictures and just as soon as I can get squared away I'm having some especially made to take care of these friends. If those who have asked for them will just bear in mind that it takes a little time for a newcomer to get his feet on the ground out here, I know they'll forgive me if I don't reply by return mail.

But enough about my mail and let's get along with my screen career.

After my studio tour, which I told you about last week, Eddie Selzer, the publicity director, collared me and told me portraits were needed to help sell "Love Is On the Air." You know, pictures have to be sold, and the only samples the salesmen have are the "stills" from the production and portraits they make in the gallery.

So we have to look as manly and virile and romantic as possible in order to coax people into the theater to see us.

Anyway, I arrived at the "portrait gallery" the next morning and found it quite a place. It has all the trimmings except a "birdie" to look at, and enough lights to make you think you are in a Turkish bath.

I found June Travis there ahead of me, perched on a stool drinking a bottle of soda pop and dressed in cool-looking slacks. Over the slacks she was wearing a smart wrap and a classy looking hat. This seemed to be slightly screwy somehow, until she explained she was making fashion pictures and the slacks wouldn't show.

After half a dozen changes of costume, the photographer went to work on me. I assumed that angle and this one while the bulb presser tried to get some art into my not too classic profile.

June and I did some high class "necking" portraits, too, that is "clinch" stuff which is supposed to make the hearts of the young beat a little faster when they see them.

That would have been fun if it hadn't been so terribly hot, and I was glad when noon came and I supposedly was free to go horseback riding with a photographer. However, they changed my mind for me again and instead of riding we wound up at a place called Pop's Willow Lake.

Which certainly is an overstatement. The "willows" are imported palm trees and as for the "lake" – well, where I come from they call puddles like that ponds and put a diving board in the deep end after they've chased the ducks away.

However, they call it a lake out here and have equipped it with everything but a dock for the steamship Queen Mary. They'd probably put that in if they figured how the big liner could get over the mountain.

To tell the truth, though, it is a nice little swimming hole and after the terrific heat of San Fernando Valley, it was a real treat. It's true what they say about sleeping under blankets and stuff like that out here. BUT it doesn't apply to the Valley, which is hemmed in by mountains and foothills, which keep out any vestige of a cool ocean breeze.

We got back to the studio about six o'clock and things were looking up. I was actually set for a several days layoff and I had just the spot picked for it. But just as I drove through the gates homeward bound, a studio cop flagged me down.

"You're due in at 8 a.m. tomorrow for added scenes on your picture," he told me.

Which introduced me to a delightful Hollywood custom. After a picture is finished and roughly cut and edited, the big bosses take a look at it and start to add little fine touches.

"I think it could be improved with a new scene here," one of them says.

"Why wouldn't it be stronger to have Reagan do this instead of that?" suggests another.

These things are talked over, writers are called in and new scenes written. The idea, of course, is sound. You never can absolutely visualize a picture story until you see it completed. Then begins the work of tightening it up, eliminating here, adding there, and, by the time they're through, they've really got something that moves and entertains.

Nick Grinde, our director, has already started on his vacation to Japan and if they hadn't caught me when they did I'd probably have been farther away than that.

Our new director, Noel Smith, was swell. The costume plot had to be rechecked a dozen times by stills and strips of film taken of previous scenes. Otherwise, we'd likely be seen entering a door in a blue suit and coming out in a grey one the next minute.

Then, too, there were new scenes that didn't fall into any of the immediately previous sequences, and for those different costumes were needed. That meant a job of collecting ties, shirts, handkerchiefs, etc., so every detail would match with the scenes taken a month ago.

Some of the added scenes were only one line, yet they required the complete re-dressing of a set – lights and equipment moved in, which meant hours of work for

only a flash or two on the screen. But that's how meticulous they are, and if anyone tells you the major studios just slap pictures together in a haphazard fashion you tell him for me he's crazy.

During my first day's work on these additional scenes I made seven costume changes. Don't get me wrong. I don't mean seven different changes, as I haven't that big a wardrobe yet. We'd shoot a series of "takes" in one set where I might wear a brown, blue, and grey suit in that order, then move to another set where I'd have to climb into the brown and start all over through the costume changing routine.

I felt like the time I had my first pair of long pants bought for me and I tried on about every suit in the store.

My biggest surprise was in remaking the very first scene of the picture, which I had put down in my memory as sort of a landmark. The producers had found they needed George E. Stone for another picture and a new player, Grant McKenzie, was substituted. That meant going all the way through, too, and making over the few scenes Stone had been in.

One of our new scenes placed me in a broadcasting studio with two children. I was curious about "baby" actors, having always wondered if they were spoiled little brats or real kids.

The little girl in the picture, a tot as cute and not much bigger than a doll, was playing in her fiftieth picture. She was completely unspoiled, and quite mature, too. I couldn't talk to her as I would ordinarily talk to a child – not that I'm given to baby talk. But she had an adult point of view in talking with grownups.

But these kids present a strange paradox. One minute I was talking with her as a fellow actor and the next she and a little boy were playing with a toy wagon and having as much fun as any two children anywhere.

I grabbed an hour off to visit the cutting rooms, which I've heard about ever since I hit Hollywood. I tracked down Doug Gould, who is doing the cutting and editing job for "Love Is On the Air," and found him in a small room completely surrounded by film – little rolls of it, hundreds of them, arranged on shelves where he can pick up the scene he needs on a moment's notice.

How any actor can get high-hat after visiting the cutting department is beyond me. Those guys have more work to do and use for brains than an actor has in a week.

Doug was in front of a Movieola, peering into the lens on the machine, watching the film, while a loudspeaker poured out the dialogue from a separate track. Suddenly he snapped the machine open, slashed a red pencil across the picture and sound track, and ran some more of the conglomeration of scenes.

While I was there, I saw him snip one word out of the soundtrack and "dub" it into another scene, and that's all in the day's work for him. Cutters have been known to put an "S" on the end of a word. I think I'll stick to acting – if they'll let me.

That's how I spent my vacation, working, but here I am again – the picture is apparently all washed up and I'm headed, I hope, for a few days off. But I'm not through the gate yet, as they say out here, and anything can happen. We'll see.

THE DES MOINES REGISTER
September 19, 1937*

Played a 'Dirty Trick' – Reagan 'Suffers' at First Preview–Slides Down Behind Seat

But Audience Breaks Into Applause

* Copyright 1937, printed with permission by *The Des Moines Register*.

By Ronald (Dutch) Reagan

HOLLYWOOD, CAL.—I've been the victim of a dirty trick – making a personal appearance at a preview of my first picture – and if I never go through another experience like that for a hundred years it will be too soon.

Without warning, I was asked by Eddie Selzer, the Warner Brothers publicity director, if I wanted to do him a favor. Being that kind of guy, I said, "Sure," and never went into the details.

He explained the manager of a theater in Huntington Park, a suburb of Los Angeles, had staged a neighborhood bathing beauty contest and wanted me to present the cup to the winner.

Even when I spotted a couple of big lights out in front of the theater and a sign over the marquee announcing "Major Studio Preview Tonight," I didn't give it a thought.

It wasn't until the main title was suddenly flashed on the screen that I realized I had been hornswoggled into not only seeing myself in "Love Is On the Air," but also that I had agreed to step up in front of that audience after it had seen my first efforts as an actor and take a chance that they'd throw anything that was loose in my direction.

When the title, "Love Is On the Air," followed with the list of the cast, came on the screen, I almost died. If I had had some warning, it might have helped.

I tried to appear nonchalant, but am sure I only looked sick. Fortunately, the theater was dark so no one knew.

It didn't help my hollow leg feeling either when a publicity man sitting beside me whispered: "This is the toughest

preview spot in the world. I've seen them boo pictures here and walk out in droves."

My sufferings increased as the picture unwound and I kept sliding down in my seat until I could scarcely see over the people in front of me.

Naturally, I saw the pictures as I knew they had been made, not as they appeared cut and edited in smooth continuity on the screen.

To me, errors which other people probably never will notice seemed to stand out like billboards and I kept wishing we could make the picture over again and correct the mistakes.

They tell me that all the tortures I went through are typical reactions everyone has when he sees his first picture in public. A guy has to have a lot of nerve, after going through that, to go out and make another one.

But I guess the feeling wears off after a while and you decide you were not so bad as you thought.

I was agreeably surprised at the finish to hear the audience burst into applause but I was still mopping my brow a few minutes later when the beauty contestants were lined up on the stage and I was called up to the microphone.

Luckily, I had spotted Eddie Acuff, my partner in the picture, seated in the audience and I dragged him along with me. With him as moral support, we clowned through the contest and got away without having anything thrown at us.

I grabbed the trade papers the first thing next morning to read the worst about myself and prepared to pack my trunk for the return trip back home.

But whether they were kidding me or not, they had nothing but words of praise.

One paper went so far as to say: "Warner Bros. have a new find in Ronald Reagan, young leading man, who promises to go places."

I'd been promising myself to forget acting and go home, but decided they didn't mean that so I guess I'll stick around and see what happens. If the studio and the fans can stand it, I certainly can, too.

THE DES MOINES REGISTER
*October 3, 1937**

Four Pictures Finished, 'Dutch' Gets a Raise, Hunts for a House

He Finds Out Why an Actor Needs 50 Suits of Clothes Eats Ham & Eggs All Morning Just to Make One Scene

By Ronald (Dutch) Reagan

HOLLYWOOD, CAL.—Well, folks, here's good news for you.

With this chapter, the Memoirs of Dutch Reagan skid to a close and just like most movie stories, there's a happy ending.

My first picture, "Love Is On the Air" was released nationally Oct. 1, three others I have played in have been given the official okay and – wonder of wonders – I've hurdled my first great Hollywood barrier: MY OPTION'S BEEN TAKEN UP.

And if you know anything about this gingerbread land, you know Option Time is as important to an actor as the State Fair is to the raiser of prize hogs.

For the benefit of those who just came in, perhaps I'd better explain this option business very briefly and then get on with my story. When the newspapers announce that "So-and-So has been signed to a long-term contract," it means that they are tied up for from three to six months definitely and up to seven years on a "maybe" basis.

If, at the end of the first three months, they decide you're not hitting the ball, they simply forget to exercise the option for your services and you're out like a light. My contract, while it runs for seven years, is on a six months' basis for the first year, and after that it's on a yearly schedule.

---

* Copyright 1937, printed with permission by *The Des Moines Register*.

While I haven't been in Hollywood six months yet, they've already notified me that they intend to keep me for the next six months' period.

Salary increases automatically go with each option so if you don't start at too little and stick it out for seven years, you're apt to be making enough money by

the end of your contract to start writing indignant letters to the newspapers about the cruel income tax. Even with luck, it will be some time before I'll feel impelled to take my pen in hand.

So far, I've "done" four pictures since landing out here in May, and I've been kept so busy that I realize now why the big stars in this racket don't want to make more than one film a year. It would be swell if you could get away with it.

The picture I'm just finishing is now called "Accidents Will Happen," but don't bet on that as the final title. It probably will be changed. The writers certainly gave me plenty to do, and I've been married, divorced, had a black eye, and been up before a judge so far – in the film, of course.

Gloria Blondell is really the girl in my life – again I'm speaking of "Accidents Will Happen" – but before she comes along I've got a wife, and so help me, you're going to want to kick her teeth out before we finally part company. Sheila Bromley plays that role, and she does such a convincing job that it took me several minutes to get over hating her after each scene we played together.

In the story, I'm an insurance adjuster trying to track down racketeers who stage fake accidents and collect from my company.

My loving wife gets tangled up with the racketeers and double crosses me out of my job. From there I go to shiny pants and soleless shoes faster than a banker in 1929, and you'll expect to hear me sing,

"Brother Can You Spare a Dime" in the next scene.

But just in time to avert that catastrophe, Gloria comes along with a pep talk and I decide to get in on the easy money. Using my knowledge gained from the insurance adjusting experience, I clean up on fake accidents so foolproof that the fakers actually feel hurt.

I wind up in cahoots with the racketeers, who framed me in the first place, but it is all part of the story and how it comes out is one of the secrets you'll have to lay your dough on the line at the box office to find out.

There's one thing I'm collecting out here besides experience and a good suntan, and that's a large wardrobe of assorted clothes and accessories.

I never used to believe the stories I read about some actor having 50 or more suits of clothes, but now I am convinced. All players cast in roles which call for modern dress are expected to supply their own clothes, and I'm no exception.

For this picture the script calls for eight complete changes, and my best friend in Hollywood right now is my tailor. I hope this friendship lasts until his bill is paid.

Every picture is a new experience and each has its problem. The very first day of "Accidents Will Happen" we did a breakfast scene that lasted most of the day. Have you ever eaten ham and eggs from 9 a.m. until 12 p.m.? Well, don't, especially when you have to go on acting in front of a plate of half-eaten food from 2 until 6 p.m.

After four hours, those once delicious eggs look a little pale around the gills – and so did I.

I mentioned a black eye a little while back. That was applied in Perc Westmore's make-up department and looked so real that I started reaching for beefsteak. Several people who should have known better wanted to know where I got my "shiner."

I wasn't always on the receiving end, though, and in one scene I was supposed to bounce one off Andy Lawlor's button. Andy is another swell fellow who can do a surprisingly good job of convincing you that he's a heel.

It's been explained before, I think, that a movie K.O. is a case of the hand being quicker than eye. The punch really whistles past the chin, the victim falls and the sound department dubs in a convincing smack and it looks and sounds like the real thing.

While we were rehearsing I wore my glasses and explained to Lawlor that I suffer from astigmatism. I further remarked that the scene worried me because without glasses I was apt to misjudge my distance and explode my manly right between his features instead of missing him.

Bill Clemons, the director, took advantage of my warning to "rib" Lawlor a bit and instructed the make-up man to stand by to fix up his face "in case of accident."

Came the moment when action was called, we spoke our few lines and I swung one from the floor. Andy didn't wait – he hit the dirt before I was within hailing distance of his jaw so we helped him up and told him we were only kidding.

With "Accidents Will Happen" finished, I'm in the market for a house and already have a list of 15 real estate agents.

I'm bringing my parents, Mr. and Mrs. John Edward Reagan, out from the

old family home in Dixon, Ill., now that it looks like I've got a permanent job – for at least six months more – and for the first time in several years I'm going to get my feet under the table and enjoy food "just like mother used to make."

And am I happy!

It's time to say goodbye for now. You'll be seeing me, I hope, and perhaps some of these days when my career is a little farther advanced, I'll take my typewriter in hand and knock off a few more letters from Hollywood.

Good luck.

> "An actor knows two important things – to be honest in what he's doing and to be in touch with the audience. That's not bad advice for a politician either. My actor's instinct simply told me to speak the truth as I saw it and felt it."

RONALD REAGAN
Conversation with speechwriter Landon Parvin, 1988

Interlude: 1947-1949

REAGAN LOOKS THE PART OF AN EXECUTIVE AT THE SCREEN ACTORS GUILD, WHERE HE SERVES SEVEN TERMS AS PRESIDENT.

(Photo courtesy of the Screen Actors Guild)

INTERLUDE: 1947-1949

After WWII, Reagan experiences a series of setbacks in his personal and professional lives. He had hoped to star in action pictures, but the studio insists that he appear in comedies and dramas. He is particularly reluctant to costar with Shirley Temple in her first adult role – because he dislikes the script and feels he is too old for the part. Jack Warner promises that if he does the Temple picture, his next movie will be a Western.

While shooting the film, *That Hagen Girl,* Reagan has to repeatedly jump into a cold river to rescue Shirley Temple (Mary Hagen) from a suicide attempt. He subsequently comes down with a raging case of viral pneumonia and spends two weeks in the hospital. The doctors consider it a miracle that he survives.

While Reagan is in Cedars of Lebanon, his wife Jane Wyman is rushed to Queen of Angels Hospital, where she delivers their daughter Christine three months prematurely. The baby dies the next day. Reagan and Jane grow increasingly apart, and separate in late 1947 – finally divorcing in mid-1948.

Reagan takes the divorce hard. He can't lose himself in his career because he's only offered parts for movies he doesn't want to make. Unlike some of his colleagues, he doesn't have the financial independence to refuse roles, go on suspension, and forego his salary. He is cash strapped now that he and Jane are living in separate households. He does his best to see the children frequently, and spends weekends with them at his ranch in Northridge and later in Malibu.

During this time, Reagan goes through a public feud with studio head Jack Warner over his belief that Warner has ruined his career, and the two old friends are at odds for years.

In 1947, Reagan is elected president of the Screen Actors Guild – a post he holds until 1952. These are the years of the Hollywood blacklist and other attempts to stem what some consider Communist influence in the movie business. While there is much disagreement about what happened and who is to blame during this period, both sides of the issue agree on one thing: these are terrible, terrible times.

Reagan's experiences during these years lead him to examine his political leanings – and contribute to his eventual move from the Democratic to Republican Party.

In 1949, Reagan meets Nancy Davis, who brings much love and happiness into his life. The same year, his agent Lew Wasserman negotiates a contract that allows Reagan to work for studios other than Warner Brothers – and he finally gets to appear in a series of Westerns. Reagan makes only one more movie for Warner Brothers – and, while it's not a Western, it's the next best thing: a sports film.

Reagan celebrates the 1949 Christmas season by helping sort packages at the Los Angeles post office. He is pictured here with postmaster Michael Fanning. Several years of personal and professional stresses — near-fatal pneumonia, the loss of a newborn, a divorce, a shattered leg that required long-term hospitalization, and career disappointments — take their toll on Reagan. He appears thin and drawn in the above photo, but his luck is about to change with a new love and new opportunities.

(UCLA Charles E. Young Research Library Department of Special Collections, Los Angeles Times Photographic Archives, Copyright © Regents of the University of California, UCLA Library)

PART III: 1950-1957

IN 1951, REAGAN PURCHASES THREE HUNDRED ACRES IN MALIBU CANYON AND NAMES HIS RANCH YEARLING ROW. THE PROPERTY — AND THE HARD PHYSICAL LABOR IT ENTAILS — BRINGS HIM MUCH FULFILLMENT, AS DO THE THOROUGHBREDS HE RAISES THERE.

Chapter Twelve
The Last Outpost

When Lew Wasserman calls with the offer, Reagan thinks it must be a joke.

"So what do you say, Ronnie?" his agent asks.

"Not a chance," Reagan replies, and then explains some of the reasons why he doesn't want to work for Bill Pine and Bill Thomas – starting with their reputation as the kings of B movies.

Pine and Thomas are infamous for their lowbrow fare about men working in dangerous occupations. Typical titles include: *Power Dive*, *Forced Landing*, *Flying Blind*, and *Wrecking Crew*. And that's definitely not the kind of picture Reagan wants to be caught dead in.

It has been a long, difficult struggle to extricate himself from his Warner Brothers contract and get the chance to make pictures at other studios. He expects Wasserman to bring him something good – not the kind of dreck that Bill Pine and Bill Thomas produce.

So far, the only deal Wasserman has made for Reagan is *Bedtime for Bonzo* – a cute picture, but nothing to earn him any awards.

Reagan will turn forty in a few months. It is make-it-or break-it time career-wise. Wasserman should know better than to entertain offers from the Dollar Bills, as Pine and Thomas are called – thanks to their reputation for penny pinching.

"Just talk to them," Wasserman says.

"I think I need to talk to a new agent," Reagan tells him.

"Ronnie, they've got a budget for this one. A million bucks," Wasserman explains.

It's common knowledge in the business that Pine and Thomas never spend more than a hundred grand on a picture.

"Are you sure you have the decimal in the right place?" Reagan replies.

"Ronnie, just do me one favor," Wasserman says in a cajoling tone. "Hear what they have to say. If it doesn't work out, you can fire me."

"You're fired now."

"It's a Western," Wasserman says in a near whisper.

The word "Western" stops Reagan. Yes, more than anything he wants to make a Western. But a low-budget, lowbrow Western isn't what he has in mind. He hopes for something grand, something uplifting, something along the lines of what his good friend John Wayne stars in – *Stagecoach*, *Red River*, *Fort Apache*.

Still, he's wanted to appear in a Western since coming to Hollywood. The closest he's come to a Western was playing a cavalry officer in *Santa Fe Trail* ten years before.

Well, maybe it is worth talking to the Dollar Bills…

A few weeks later, Reagan is driving to Arizona, following a horse trailer carrying his prized mare, Baby. The Dollar Bills clinched the deal, when they agreed to ship her to the location and allow Reagan to ride her in the movie. Yep, a month in the great outdoors riding Baby will more than compensate for any shortcomings of this particular horse opera.

The Last Outpost is shot in the desert outside Tucson, Arizona, an area famous for its tall saguaro cacti.
(University of Chicago photographic archive)

As Reagan travels east on Highway 10, he thinks about his drive from Des Moines to Los Angeles in 1937, thirteen years before. He remembers his high expectations and high spirits on the road. Now he is older and he hopes a bit wiser. But one thing hasn't changed – his awe at America's natural wonders. Right now, he is enjoying the austere beauty of the desert – the cliffs, the canyons, the cacti.

He drives slowly, right behind Baby's trailer, bringing up the rear, protecting his most prized possession. He doesn't know how he could have endured the past two years, since his divorce from Jane, if it hadn't been for Baby – and, of course, the children. But now something has changed – a glimmer of hope in a lovely woman named Nancy Davis, whom he'd met about a year before. The relationship is new and he is still gun-shy, but Nancy is the first woman since his divorce with whom he feels totally at ease.

When he arrives at the location near Tombstone, Arizona, about seventy miles southeast of Tucson, he parks behind Baby's trailer. He could not feel prouder of her. She is a beautiful thoroughbred with a sweet nature, high intelligence, and amazing adaptability and stamina. He just knows the horse wranglers on this picture will fall in love with her.

But when he guides Baby out of the trailer, instead of the "oohs" and "aahs" he'd expected, he hears snickers and rude comments.

"She won't last a day in this heat."

"Pack her up and send her home."

"She's a powder puff."

Reagan is confident his horse, Baby, can outshine the professional movie equines.

Reagan feels his face flush. He has a temper – one he usually tries to keep under wraps. But he has trouble controlling his feelings when anybody hurts or insults someone or something he loves.

"Want to bet?" Reagan says to a weathered-looking cowpoke standing in front of the other horse wranglers.

"Yep," the man says, and then proceeds to explain that he's reviewed five hundred horses for two hundred parts in the movie. "And, believe me," he says, "that spoiled princess ain't going to make the cut."

Reagan turns and looks into Baby's eyes – and he's sure she understood everything the man has just said.

"My horse can outrun and outlast any horse in this picture."

The man bursts out laughing, slaps his knee, and ambles away shaking his head.

Reagan knows Baby will show them all. He decides to let the matter drop for now.

After turning over Baby to a groom for feed and water, Reagan reports to a trailer for his wardrobe fitting. His costar Bruce Bennett, who plays his brother in the picture, is standing there in his Union Army blues.

Reagan has met Bennett on a number of occasions over the years and has always liked him. But during the past few years, Reagan has felt resentful each time he's thought of Bruce Bennett – a man who had done nothing wrong, except portray a character that Reagan had been dying to play. After Reagan turned down the role of Cody in *The Treasure of the Sierra Madre* at Jack Warner's insistence, John Huston had cast Bennett in the part.

It is a bitter memory and Reagan hopes he won't think of it every time he sees Bennett during the next month.

Putting on the uniform brings up another bad memory for Reagan. When he met with Pine and Thomas, they promised him a real Western. But when the script arrived, it was another cavalry picture – just like *Santa Fe Trail*. This isn't what he means by a Western. A Western has lawmen, cattle rustlers, saloons, marshals, sheriffs, gunslingers.

This is a saga about the Civil War. And while Reagan is a Civil War buff and served many years in the U.S. Cavalry, this isn't the kind of picture he hoped to make when he left Warners.

Reagan tries on his Confederate Army grays and he and Bennett stand beside each other looking in a full-length mirror. They will play brother against brother in the movie.

The picture is called *The Last Outpost*. Set in 1862, the plot revolves around troops of Union and Confederate soldiers fighting over supply trains and gold – and finally joining together to fend off the Apaches.

Reagan and Bruce Bennett play brothers on opposite sides during the Civil War.
(Author collection)

Besides getting to ride Baby and working outdoors, there is another big plus to this picture – Reagan's costar, Rhonda Fleming. They strike up an instant friendship, thanks to a mutual interest – both are friends of Nancy Davis. Soon Reagan begins to feel protective toward Rhonda, as if she's a younger sister. All the men on the picture seem to be in love with her. And who can blame them? Rhonda is one of the most beautiful women in the world. She has the whole package – face, figure, talent, plus a good heart and a strong faith in God.

In *The Last Outpost,* where Reagan ends up wearing both Confederate and Yankee uniforms, Rhonda Fleming plays his love interest. They go on to make three more movies for Pine and Thomas. Fleming remembers, "I had just met him when they paired us together for our first film. Of our four films, I believe he was at his best in *The Last Outpost* on his horse and in command – I could see, looking back, his future strength as a leader...he was a natural. I had no idea in our many love scenes that I was kissing the future president of the United States."

(Author collection)

The Bills are models of efficiency. For years, they've been saying, "We don't want to make pictures that cost a million dollars. We want to make pictures that look like a million dollars." Well, Reagan figures, now that they have a million-dollar budget the two men will have to say their pictures look like ten million dollars' worth.

At lunchtime on the first day's shoot, Reagan wanders over to check on Baby and take her for a trot. But the Bills corral him to a tent where they tell him it's a command performance to show up for lunch.

"I'm not very hungry," Reagan says.

"Well, you don't have to eat," Pine says, furrowing his bushy eyebrows, "but you have to show up."

"Don't worry, I'll be back on time," Reagan says, heading toward the horse stable.

From left: The Dollar Bills, Bill Thomas and Bill Pine, in a pensive mood – trying to think up new ways to save money.

"Sorry, Ronnie," Thomas tells him, running a hand through his thinning blond hair, "Wasserman should have told you that on our pictures everybody goes to lunch together."

"We need to make sure everybody comes back at the same time," Pine explains. "That's one of the ways we keep costs down."

As they walk toward the lunchroom, Reagan takes the opportunity to give the Bills a suggestion for improving the script. Bill Thomas takes a pen and notebook out of his back pocket and jots down some notes. "Great idea, Ronnie. Consider it done." Hey, Reagan thinks, these guys are growing on me.

Reagan has to hand it to the Dollar Bills. They are a couple of hardworking, hard-driving guys – and, despite their penny-pinching ways, they pay well and serve a first-rate lunch.

While shooting *The Last Outpost* during October and November 1950, Reagan stays in Tucson's historic Santa Rita Hotel and writes to Nancy on hotel stationery.

In the evenings back in Tucson, Reagan goes to a movie almost every night. When he gets back to his hotel room, he feels lonely and realizes how much he misses Nancy. He wants to write her a letter every night, but is still concerned about getting too serious – and when you send a letter to a girlfriend, it usually means she's your one and only.

But after about a week, he breaks down and addresses an envelope to Miss Nancy Davis, 941-½ Hilgard, Westwood Village, L.A., Calif. As he waits on the set between scenes, he unfolds a piece of hotel stationery and jots down a few words.

> *Dear Nancy,*
>
> *Just a quick line from somewhere south of Tucson (pronounced Tooson). I'm balancing this on my knee while I wait to ride gallantly over another hill. I know why the Confederates lost – they were so d__n hot in these uniforms they couldn't fight.*

He knows the letter's opening paragraph will make Nancy laugh. Before he realizes it, he's telling her about more serious matters – how three stuntmen have been injured, how dangerous the work is for all the actors, and how he's contracted the Arizona version of Montezuma's revenge. Nancy wasn't keen on him going away for a month, and this letter will let her know he's not having too much fun while on location.

Nancy Davis is an up-and-coming Hollywood starlet when she meets Ronald Reagan in 1949.
(Photo: Reagan Library)

The shooting days are long and hot – and very, very tiring. On most days, the two hundred chosen steeds are wilting by noon and worn out by early afternoon. Baby is the exception. She not only endures, she thrives – and looks as fresh in the evening as she did in the morning. Reagan feels like a proud papa – that's a thoroughbred for you.

He waits for the horse wrangler to offer some words of apology or admiration toward Baby, but the man slithers away like a sidewinder any time he sees Reagan approach.

"That's okay, Baby," Reagan whispers in his horse's ear. "You know and I know you're the best."

Baby comes through the shoot with flying colors, making Reagan feel like a proud papa.

The cast and crew gets a surprise visitor one day – Dan E. Garvey, governor of Arizona. Pine and Thomas give Garvey the speed tour – after all, nothing can stop production. Reagan chats with Garvey for a while, and they exchange a few stories about campaigning for Harry Truman in 1948.

Dan E. Garvey is governor of Arizona during the making of *The Last Outpost*. When Garvey shows up on set, he finds himself in a new role.

The Last Outpost's rousing story inspires a Fawcett Movie Comic.

The Last Outpost Fawcett Movie Comic features remarkable likenesses of Bruce Bennett (left) and Ronald Reagan (right).

Garvey asks Reagan about the picture and reveals he's a Civil War buff. Reagan thinks it would be great if Garvey appeared as an extra in the movie – and excuses himself to track down Pine and Thomas.

When Reagan shares his idea with the producers, Pine slaps him on the back, and Thomas says, "You're worth every penny we're paying you, Ronnie," which Reagan considers high praise coming from the two most frugal men in the business. Thomas adds, "It wouldn't surprise me if you end up as governor yourself one day."

To this, Reagan just smiles. It isn't the first time someone has suggested he enter politics. But he has no interest in pursuing a career in government. He just wants to make Westerns!

By the time the picture wraps a week before Thanksgiving, Reagan is a total convert to the bible according to Pine and Thomas. These guys are masters of minutiae, and represent the essence of free enterprise: work hard, work smart, and reap the rewards.

After *The Last Outpost* is released in April 1951, the work starts all over again. The Bills book the picture across the country – anywhere and everywhere, screening the movie in church basements, town halls, 4-H Clubs, you name it.

At one event, as Reagan walks through the door of a high school auditorium, he hears squeals from the female fans with cries of: "It's Ronald Reagan."

Next, gorgeous Rhonda Fleming glides through the door to cries of: "It's Rhonda Fleming."

When the two Dollar Bills enter, it's to shouts of: "It's nobody."

As Reagan tours the country promoting the movie, he learns to appreciate the Bills. They are nothing like the self-described geniuses or pretentious poseurs that infect Hollywood. These guys are yeomen, down-to-earth realists – the kind of people who built America and made it great.

As he signs autographs and shakes hands with fans, people who spent their hard-earned money to see the picture, for the first time in a long time Reagan feels good about what he does for a living. He truly believes that, more than anything, people want to see movies filled with action and adventure – stories that are uplifting, exciting, and inspiring. And, from now on, that's the only kind of picture he intends to make.

Reagan feels a bit guilty about misjudging Pine and Thomas – how wrong he was. These two paid him well, respected his ideas, and put him in a big-budget action picture. What more could he ask from a producer?

HOW HOLLYWOOD PREPARED RONALD REAGAN FOR THE WORLD STAGE: While working on *The Last Outpost*, Reagan understands that good leaders – such as Pine and Thomas – lead by example and show their leadership by getting results: a good product, on budget, on time, with workers that enjoy the process. Sounds like a fine way to run a business – or a government.

Ronald Reagan and Rhonda Fleming star in four movies together and enjoy mutual respect and appreciation. Rhonda Fleming inscribed this still from *The Last Outpost* to wish her costar a happy 100th birthday in 2011. "We miss you, Ronnie. Thinking of you on your 100th birthday. Love Rhonda Fleming."

(Photo courtesy of Rhonda Fleming)

HAPPY DAYS ARE HERE AGAIN —

PERSONALLY AND PROFESSIONALLY.

(Author collection)

Chapter Thirteen
THE WINNING TEAM

"Ronnie, I think we've found a part you're going to really like," Jack Warner says over the phone. It's November 1951.

Reagan is at Yearling Row, his ranch in Malibu, and he's just come inside after a long day of digging fence posts. He adores the place, so his heart is really in his work and everything is a labor of love.

He sits down and waits for Warner to explain what he has in mind – and expects the usual: a light comedy or a maudlin melodrama.

"What is it?" Reagan says. *"John and Mary Have a Baby,* or *Night Unto Naught?"*

"I promised we'd find you a real Ronald Reagan picture."

"Jack, you've been promising that for over a dozen years."

"How'd you like to play a pitcher?"

"What kind of a picture?"

"I said pitcher."

"Who's on first?"

"It's the part of Grover Cleveland Alexander," Warner says, naming one of the all-time great baseball pitchers.

"I thought you gave that part to Steve Cochran," Reagan replies. He'd heard Cochran talking about the role when they'd made *Storm Warning* the previous year.

There is a pause at Warner's end of the phone that makes Reagan think the line has gone dead.

Steve Cochran, pictured at left in 1946, lost the role of baseball pitcher Grover Cleveland Alexander after bragging to the press that he knew little about the great American pastime.

"Hello," Reagan says.

"I'm here."

"So what happened?"

Warner explains that Cochran had recently spouted some ill-considered comments to the press. He'd given an interview admitting he didn't know much about baseball, but neither did Gary Cooper and Coop did all right as Lou Gehrig in *Pride of the Yankees*.

"We took him off the pitcher...I mean, picture," Warner says.

Reagan wishes he were independently wealthy, so he could just run the ranch, breed his thoroughbreds, and build some fences. But he has to work to keep everything going.

"Send over the script," Reagan says.

"You're going to be crazy about it," Warner tells him.

After he reads the script, Reagan can't say he's crazy about it – sections are too schmaltzy for his taste – but he loves the idea of playing a baseball hero. He has always been a sports nut, and the greatest joy of his career was playing George "The Gipper" Gipp in *Knute Rockne: All American*.

Reagan wants to look believable and not rely on a double, so he puts out the word that he wants a major leaguer to coach him. "The best guy you can get," he explains.

Reagan gets what he asked for and more in Bob Lemon, the leading pitcher in the National League. They decide to meet on the Warner back lot Monday through Friday for six weeks and practice throwing two hours each day.

Reagan and Lemon are about the same age and have similar personalities – laid back and lighthearted – and they hit it off big time. Lemon tells Reagan he's going to show him the difference between throwing from the mound and just throwing.

When they take breaks, Reagan and Lemon share stories about their backgrounds, their families, and the things that matter to them. Reagan tells Lemon about playing The Gipper, and gushes about his girlfriend, Nancy Davis.

Reagan learns that Lemon lives in Long Beach during the off-season and plays golf nearly every day.

"Well, let's get started," Reagan suggests, "so you can get in at least nine holes."

"Do you play?" Lemon asks.

"I prefer horses," Reagan responds.

"Santa Anita?" Lemon guesses, naming a racetrack north of Los Angeles.

"No," Reagan says, "Yearling Row," naming his ranch.

Reagan explains about the ranch and his thoroughbreds, then picks up a baseball. He waits for Lemon to tell him what to do, but Lemon just says, "Throw me the ball."

Reagan winds up and tosses one overhand into Lemon's glove. Lemon explains that he wanted to see how Reagan naturally threw the ball so he could know where to start.

Two hours later, Reagan is pitching less like an amateur and more like a pro, at least in terms of technique.

"It's all in the practice," Lemon says.

"Six weeks to go," Reagan says as they shake hands to end the day's session and Lemon speeds off to his waiting golf game.

On the way home from Burbank, Reagan swings by Westwood to see his personal passion – Nancy Davis, the lovely starlet he's been dating for a few years. When Reagan tells her about his latest picture, Nancy shouts "whoopee." It turns out she's been crazy for baseball from the womb. The story goes that her mother's due date was July 4, 1921. But Edith was such an avid baseball fan that she didn't want to miss a Yankees' doubleheader. So she postponed Nancy's birth by two days.

Nancy spends every weekend with Reagan and the children – Maureen, who's almost eleven and Michael, almost seven. He and Nancy make the ninety-minute drive out to the kids' boarding school in Palos Verdes and then travel back to the Malibu ranch. On the long drives, they sing and play games – and everyone gets along like one happy family.

Reagan is delighted to learn that his friend Doris Day – costar in the previous year's *Storm Warning* – will play Aimee Alexander, Grover Cleveland Alexander's devoted wife. Reagan feels lucky to have such wonderful female companionship on screen and off. The best part is that Nancy and Doris are both big-time baseball fans – and can rattle off statistics at a pace that most sports writers can't match.

When the shoot begins, Reagan thinks Doris is doing a fine job with her role – actually, it is her picture, which tells Grover Cleveland Alexander's story from his wife's perspective. Together, Aimee and Alex are a winning team. Doris is pert and perky, with a depth of dedication and concern that touches Reagan.

Grover Cleveland Alexander, pictured above, was one of the all-time greatest baseball pitchers. As of 2010, his ninety shutouts remain a National League Record. He is tied for most wins at 373, and holds many other records. When he was born in 1887, his mother named him after the then-president of the United States. His presidential connection continued when future president Ronald Reagan portrayed him in *The Winning Team*. Alexander played for the Chicago Cubs, Philadelphia Phillies, and St. Louis Cardinals. Reagan felt a special connection to Alexander because of their mutual involvement with the Cubs – Alexander as a player and Reagan as an announcer. Alexander died in 1950, two years before Warner Brothers produced *The Winning Team*.

But there are a few things about his own role that Reagan would like to change. He goes to the director, Lewis Seiler, and expresses his misgivings about the script – saying he has a hard time believing that Alex spoke in such an uneducated manner, and that it would be a disservice to Alex's memory to portray him this way. Before he can finish making his points, the director cuts him off, saying the real Mrs. Grover Cleveland Alexander read the script and approved the dialogue. Score: Seiler, 1; Reagan, 0.

Okay, Reagan can live with delivering ungrammatical lines. His next issue is much more significant – the screenplay fails to mention Alex's epilepsy and leads people to believe all his problems stemmed from getting beaned a few times. The director tells Reagan that the Studio and Mrs. Alexander nixed any specific references to Alexander's condition. The best they can do is make a few broad hints about blackouts.

Reagan feels miserable that they can't speak directly about Alex's epilepsy. Getting the story – the real story – out there could help remove the stigma associated with the illness.

From time to time, Reagan thinks about what happened his last time at bat. At a charity baseball game in July 1949, a jokester tripped him and he ended up with multiple breaks in his right leg. He spent months in St. John's Hospital flat on his back with his leg in traction and then spent a year on crutches. Well, as the old saying goes, you gotta get back in the saddle.

Reagan knows he's a better football player than baseball player – even though he was on the all-star baseball team in high school and college. He even played in Galesburg, where Grover Cleveland Alexander got his start. Strange coincidence, but Reagan's life is full of them.

The shoot begins in the middle of December 1951. They film the indoor scenes at Warner Brothers in Burbank and the outdoor scenes at the Iverson Movie Ranch in Chatsworth, California – the site of thousands of action pictures.

While making the movie, Reagan not only gets a lot of throwing practice, he also gets plenty of practice chewing gum. He stuffs five pieces in his mouth before every scene where Grover Cleveland Alexander pitches a game. Unlike most of his teammates, Alexander didn't chew tobacco, but went through lots of Juicy Fruit during each day at the ballpark. Reagan learns all this from Aimee Alexander, who is on set for every scene – offering insights into Alexander's habits, behavior, and manner of speaking.

Bob Lemon (left) – a veteran pitcher with the Cleveland Indians – shows Ronald Reagan the proper pitching form in one of their many practice sessions. Lemon coaches Reagan for six weeks leading up to the December 15, 1951 start date for *The Winning Team*. One of baseball's most respected pitchers, Lemon enjoys 207 career wins and in 1976 is inducted into the Baseball Hall of Fame.

(Photo: Associated Press)

Doris Day as Aimee Alexander and Ronald Reagan as Grover Cleveland Alexander in *The Winning Team*, which is shot at Warner Brothers in Burbank and at the Iverson Movie Ranch in Chatsworth, California. The picture is the duo's second outing together – after the previous year's *Storm Warning*. Prior to these roles, Day had appeared in musicals and was mainly known as a singer. In her pictures with Reagan, Day got the chance to show she was more than just a pretty face and a pretty voice – she was also a serious actress. Day and Reagan dated briefly following his divorce and remained friends. She later wrote of him: "There were two things about Ronnie that impressed me: how much he liked to dance and how much he liked to talk. I remember telling him that he should be touring the country making speeches. He was very good at it...he had what I would call a political personality – engaging, strong, and very voluble."

(Photo courtesy doctormacro.com)

One day, during a particularly intense scene, where Alex refuses to tell Aimee the source of his problem and allows her to think he is just a common drunk, Reagan hears laughter ring out on the set. He feels angry and humiliated. Here he was acting his heart out in a dramatic scene and someone laughed. The director yells, "Cut," then turns and glares at the crew.

"Who was it?" Seiler says.

A grip waves a piece of newspaper as if it's a white flag.

"I'm sorry, boss," the man says, "but this is a scream."

The cast and crew huddle around the man, trying to get a look at the paper. People rip it out of each other's hands. Finally Reagan storms over to the crowd, grabs the sheet and in a few seconds is laughing, too.

"What's it say?" people want to know.

"Here," Reagan says, "let me read it to you."

And in his most actorly voice – the voice that gained him a job announcing for the Cubs and the voice that caught the attention of casting director Max Arnow – Reagan reads what's written on the paper.

"Louis Hippe, owner of shortwave radio station W6APQ in North Hollywood intercepted a message delivered in English over a Moscow station. The Russian announcer said: Hollywood is creating a propaganda film called *The Winning Team* to glorify a group of Yankee murderers."

At this, everyone starts to howl, realizing that the Russians have interpreted "Yankee" to mean "imperialist" and "murderers" for "murderers' row" – a group of power hitters from the 1927 team that included Lou Gehrig and Babe Ruth. The message intercepted over the shortwave radio is typical Russian propaganda. It is January 1951 and the cold war between the U.S. and Russia is pure frost.

Reagan has lots of laughs on the set with Bob Lemon, who acts as Reagan's double in long shots, and plays a role as team member Jesse Haines. In one crucial scene, Alexander – trying for a comeback – nails a catcher's mitt to the side of a barn, and then practices pitching into it.

The director, Lewis Seiler, intends to shoot the scenes from behind, using Lemon as a double for Alexander. He figures Lemon will be able to sink a few into the mitt, and they can move on to other scenes.

"Throw it down the middle," Seiler calls.

Lemon throws and keeps throwing, but can't seem to hit the mark. After numerous vain attempts, Reagan says, "Mind if I try?"

Lemon shoots him a skeptical look but tosses him the ball, saying, "Be my guest."

Reagan winds up, throws, and bingo, gets the ball right in the mitt. Lemon tosses his hat on the ground and stomps on it.

"It's all your fault, Bob," Reagan says. "You're just too good of a teacher."

By the time the shoot ends in mid-January 1952, Reagan and Nancy have grown closer. She takes an active interest in the ranch – something the kids love because she ends up doing many of their chores, including helping Reagan with the fences and his other building projects.

Soon after the picture wraps, Reagan takes Nancy for dinner at Chasen's, where she drops a bombshell.

"I'm thinking about asking my agent to find me a play in New York," she says.

Reagan gulps. He knows he absolutely can't live without Nancy. She is the love and the light of his life.

"I think we should get married," he says.

Nancy tells him she thinks so, too.

The wedding date is set for Tuesday, March 4, 1952 at the Little Brown Church in the Valley, followed by a reception at the Toluca Lake, California, home of Reagan's long-time friend William Holden and his wife Ardis, who serve as witnesses during the wedding ceremony.

After a trip to Phoenix, Arizona, to meet Nancy's parents, Reagan is back at work for the two Bills – Pine and Thomas – making *Tropic Zone*, again costarring Rhonda Fleming. When the shoot ends in April, Reagan is delighted to learn that he and Nancy are expecting a baby at the end of the year.

In early June 1952, Reagan and his new bride hop aboard the Southern Pacific's Sunset Limited and head east for a special celebration – the premiere of *The Winning Team* in Springfield, Missouri. Reagan has always been a train buff, and he's excited to share his love for rail travel with Nancy. He points out sites along the way – the desert, the mountains, wildlife, wildflowers – and as always Nancy gives him her complete attention. She never complains, even though a bumpy train ride isn't the most comfortable way to travel while you're pregnant. Nancy is a real sport, a true companion, a perfect wife.

Reagan's favorite lines from *The Winning Team* are: "God must think a lot of me to have given me you." That's exactly how he feels about Nancy. He is so very, very grateful to have her love and to have her in his life.

Ronald Reagan and Nancy Davis engagement photo, January 1952.
(Photo: Reagan Library)

The new Mr. and Mrs. Ronald W. Reagan cut the cake on March 4, 1952.
(Photo: Reagan Library)

The train ride seems like another honeymoon and Reagan definitely feels like a newlywed – giddy and in love. Reagan has plenty of experience as a narrator and he can't help himself – he lends his voiceover to the scenery all the way to San Antonio. There, they change to The Texas Special, where they're guests in a luxury car owned by the man who heads the Frisco Rail Line.

Reagan feels as if he and Nancy are traveling in a small palace as they glide toward Springfield, Missouri. The gentle rocking of the rail car is so comforting, and all is right with the world as they move toward the heartland in this bright red train.

The slow travel gives Reagan and Nancy time to enjoy each other's company, hold hands, talk about their plans for the future, pick out baby names, and take in the wonder and the beauty of America out the window of their private car.

The trip has been so blissful and peaceful that Reagan hopes to hold onto the feeling now that the train is chugging into the Frisco Rail Station in Springfield on Thursday night, June 5th. He knows someone will be there to pick them up and figures he and Nancy will be quickly whisked to their hotel, where they can relax and get ready for bed.

Reagan and Nancy board The Texas Special in San Antonio, Texas -- and enjoy a private luxury Pullman rail car that belongs to the owner of the Frisco Rail Line. The Texas Special is a beautiful train – bright red with a white star in front to symbolize the Lone Star state.

(Photo courtesy Springfield-Green County Library.)

When the train pulls into the station, Reagan hears what sounds like yelling and screaming outside. Nancy gazes up at him with a worried expression. He pokes his head outside their compartment and finds other members of the Hollywood contingent trying to figure out what the noise is all about.

It's after 10:30 on a sweltering summer night when Reagan, Nancy, and other members of their party stand on the rear platform of the rail car and learn that they're the cause of the uproar.

The train platform is thronged with what looks like a thousand people, who are jumping up and down with excitement to see the guests arrive in Springfield. Reagan and his wife and all the others in the rail car appear stunned at this enthusiastic welcome – especially since it's so late on a hot night. The Springfield natives make Reagan feel loved and appreciated – and most of all welcome.

After delivering some impromptu remarks to the excited crowd, several porters whisk Reagan and Nancy to a waiting Cadillac convertible, where their young driver introduces himself as, "Edwin Rice. But folks call me Cookie."

As they drive the short distance to the hotel, Reagan puts his arm around Nancy, and they both lean back and look up at the stars. Reagan realizes there's nothing like having the top down to make you feel connected to your surroundings – in this case, the heart of America.

A newspaper photo captures the delighted smiles of the Hollywood contingent. A caption accompanies the photo: "THE STARS ARRIVE – While some 750 enthusiastic movie fans crowded around for close-up views, these five distinguished Hollywood visitors and the widow of one of baseball's all-time greats stood on the platform of their special railroad car to greet Springfieldians last night."

(*Springfield Leader & Press*, June 6, 1952)

Young Mr. Rice, who reveals he's a sophomore in college, informs the Reagans that they have to make a detour before going to the hotel. He tells them they're honored guests at an outdoor square dance.

Even though Reagan and Nancy are worn out from the nearly four-day train trip, they both smile and act as if a square dance is just what they've been hoping for.

Finally, around midnight, Cookie Rice chauffeurs the Reagans to the Kentwood Arms Hotel, where all the Hollywood people are staying. Rice tells them it's the best hotel in the state.

The next morning is a whirlwind of activity – a chamber of commerce-sponsored breakfast, a press conference, a visit to a hospital polio unit, a rehearsal for the evening's festivities, and a Kiwanis Club luncheon. Wherever they go, a motorcycle policeman with his siren a-squealing leads their car.

After a nonstop morning, the Reagans retreat to their hotel room, where they have a couple of hours to relax and get ready for the four o'clock President's Premiere – a showing of *The Winning Team* at the Gillioz and Fox Theatres for members of the 35th Division National Guard and special invited guests. The division, which served with honor during WWI, is holding its annual reunion in Springfield – with its most esteemed member, President Harry Truman, in attendance.

When they arrive at the Gillioz Theatre in their convertible, they get a full view of the mob scene that awaits. Springfield has never seen anything like this – a real movie premiere with real movie stars.

The women squeal for him – and he feels shy and sheepish. After all, he is forty-one years old – too old to cause girls to swoon. Anyway, he's a married man – and a happy one at that.

The crowd – men, women, young, and old – cheer and clap when he and Nancy get out of the convertible. Reagan has never seen so many animated, excited faces at any premiere he's attended over the years – and that's fifteen years' worth of pictures.

It is nearly four o'clock on a scorching hot summer day, with the sun beating down, but people are braving the heat just for a glimpse of Reagan and his wife. Reagan is heartened by this warm – in more ways than one – reception and feels hopeful that the movie will revitalize his career.

He would like to spend more time outside waving to the crowd and signing autographs, but he's concerned about Nancy in this blistering temperature.

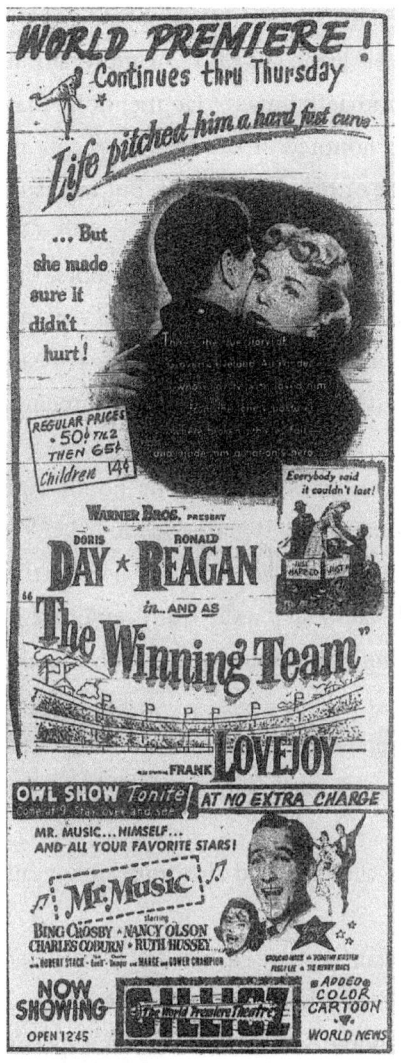

After a few more waves, smiles, and nods to the screaming, cheering crowd, Reagan ushers Nancy into the cool bliss of the air conditioned Gillioz Theatre – an ornately adorned movie palace that is opulent with a capital "O."

Reagan and Nancy wait in a private room while the moviegoers – almost twelve hundred of them – take their seats. From a spot behind the stage, Reagan and Nancy can hear the spirited chatter of the crowd. Reagan can sense the audience's excitement and anticipation – and feels uplifted by the atmosphere of fun and elation and enjoyment. By the look in Nancy's big brown eyes, he knows she's feeling what he's feeling.

At four p.m. on the dot, Reagan and Nancy take the stage and everybody in the audience stands up and begins to wave and cheer. Reagan and Nancy wave back with one hand and keep another arm around each other. They smile into the crowd, two people smiling to over a thousand, and it's as if the whole world is contained in this room and everything and anything that is happening on earth is occurring right here in Springfield at the Gillioz Theatre.

The Kentwood Arms Hotel, where the Reagans stay during their visit to Springfield, Missouri.
(Springfield-Greene County Public Library.)

When the clapping and foot stomping finally die down, Springfield Mayor Karchmer introduces Reagan and Nancy. Reagan shares a few words of appreciation to the people of Springfield for hosting this movie premiere. He mentions that Grover Cleveland Alexander would have been honored at this hearty reception. In fact, Reagan feels humbled at portraying one of his idols on film. But this isn't the first time Alexander the Great has appeared here on the screen, he reveals. On opening night in 1926, Reagan explains, when the Gillioz opened its doors, the program featured a newsreel where Grover Cleveland Alexander appeared striking out Tony Lazzeri and winning the World Series for the St. Louis Cardinals. Reagan then tells the crowd not to take his word for it, but to hear all about it from someone who was there.

"Ladies and gentlemen, boys and girls," Reagan says, "it is my honor and pleasure to present Aimee Alexander, the true star of *The Winning Team*."

Mrs. Alexander, a lovely woman in her fifties, comes out from behind the curtains and waves to the crowd. Reagan and Nancy step away from center stage as Mrs. Alexander says a few words – explaining how pleased she is with Ronald Reagan's portrayal of her husband.

"Mr. Reagan is very, very good as a ballplayer," says Mrs. Alexander. "I watched him pitch for three straight hours in one scene. But he's very modest about the whole thing."

This sends the crowd into more bursts of clapping and cheering. "Ray-gun! Ray-gun! Ray-gun!" people shout.

After Mrs. Alexander finishes her remarks, dancer Gene Nelson and his partner Virginia Gibson take the stage for a dancing exhibition. As soon as the dancing begins, ushers lead the Reagans and Mrs. Alexander to a waiting car, which speeds them to the Fox Theater just a few blocks away. There, they repeat their remarks to an equally enthusiastic crowd.

Finally, Reagan and Nancy take their seats in a balcony box seat. They hold hands as they wait for the curtains to part and the movie to begin. Reagan feels perfectly happy – personally and professionally. He is with the woman of his dreams – and about to see himself in a dream role.

The movie flies by before he knows it. All he really recalls is Nancy squeezing his hand at the picture's most dramatic moments. He feels overjoyed at the audience's reception to the movie. People stand up and cheer and he half expects men to lift him onto their shoulders and parade him through the streets of Springfield.

It's a mad rush to get out of the theater, and nearly six o'clock by the time they get outside to Rice's convertible. Police clear the streets for their car to pass and Rice delivers them back to the hotel, where they have just enough time to change into evening attire and freshen up and then it's back to the convertible and a return trip to the Gillioz for two shows and the Fox for two shows.

The evening showings are like the afternoon showings, only people are more dressed up and there seems to be an even bigger crush of spectators. It is clear that this is the biggest thing that's happened in Springfield, Missouri, since Wild Bill Hickok and Wyatt Earp rolled into town nearly a hundred years before.

After the show, Rice piles the Reagans into his Cadillac and flies them over to the Shrine Mosque for the President's Ball in honor of Harry Truman and the 35th Division of the National Guard – men who had served with valor when the U.S. joined into the fighting during World War I (1917-1919). The group is holding its annual reunion on the same weekend of *The Winning Team* premiere.

The organizers ask Reagan to say a few words to commemorate the event – and he is honored to speak before President Truman and other distinguished guests. He's met the president several times before, when campaigning for the Democratic ticket during the 1948 election. In a few months Truman will run against a strong Republican opponent – WWII hero, General Dwight D. Eisenhower. Truman is shoring up support to give a strong push against his well-liked rival.

Ronald Reagan (left) addresses distinguished guests, including President Harry S. Truman (third from right), at the Shrine Mosque in Springfield, Missouri, on June 6, 1952. Who would have guessed that less than thirty years in the future, the presidential seal would belong to Ronald W. Reagan?

(Courtesy Harry Truman Library; photo source unknown.)

By 10:30, Reagan and Nancy are back at the Kentwood Arms Hotel for another reception, where a local industrialist named Lester Cox presents Reagan with an "Ozark Hillbilly Award." In accepting the award, Reagan says: "We're all from places like Illinois and Indiana and Missouri, and we're trying to be good citizens." He tells the crowd that he will forever treasure the Hillbilly Award as a souvenir of his visit.

The next morning, a bellhop delivers the *Springfield Daily News* to the Reagans' room. A movie critic named Dale Freeman describes the movie premiere from the day before – calling Reagan's acting the "homey, I'm-like-the-neighbor-next-door type" that he has used to his advantage for a long, long time.

Edwin "Cookie" Rice was a twenty-year-old college student when his neighbor asked him if he'd like to drive some visitors around town in a Cadillac convertible. Rice ended up chauffeuring a future president while passing the current president – Harry Truman (in white hat) – in the reviewing stand during the parade in Springfield, Missouri, on June 7, 1952. Rice obtained this photo from the *Springfield News-Leader*. Thirty years later, after Reagan was elected president, Rice asked his congressman to request that Reagan sign the photo.

(Photo courtesy of Edwin "Cookie" Rice)

Nancy Reagan wrote this thank you note to Edwin Cookie Rice for acting as guide and driver during their visit to Springfield, Missouri, in June 1952. *"To Cookie. Thanks for everything. Hope we meet again. Till then lots of luck. Nancy Davis Reagan & Ronald Reagan."* Rice went on to head his family business, Ozarks Coca-Cola/Dr. Pepper Bottling Company.

(Courtesy of Edwin "Cookie" Rice; used by permission of Nancy Reagan)

Saturday, June 7, 1952, is a scorcher in Springfield. Reagan and Nancy are scheduled to ride in the convertible for a three-mile parade in downtown Springfield to honor the 35th Division of the National Guard. Reagan is concerned about Nancy sitting in an open car on such an oppressively hot day, but his wife insists that she wants to be at his side and she will be fine. Reagan tries to talk her into staying in their air-conditioned hotel room, but Nancy won't hear of it. Besides, how long can it take to drive three miles?

When Nancy climbs into the back seat, she sits up on the rear deck and gets some welcome back support. She tells her husband this is the best she's felt in weeks.

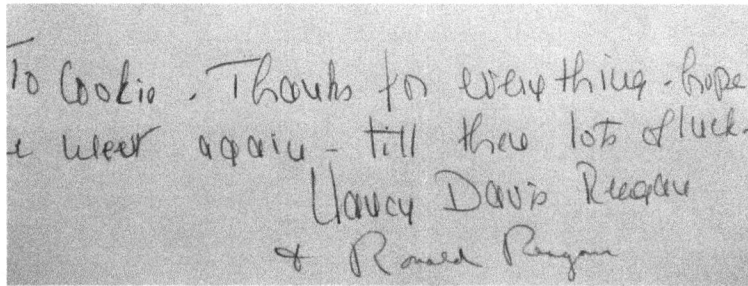

The West African nation of Gambia honored Reagan's performance as Grover Cleveland Alexander by issuing a special postage stamp.

While they inch forward, Reagan and Nancy smile and wave to the crowd – and what a crowd! There are two hundred and fifty thousand people – about twice the size of the entire population of Springfield.

As they drive past the eager, earnest faces edging the street, Reagan thinks: This is what I love about this country. All that is good, true, and beautiful about America is right here: Good people, with good values, having a good time. At this moment, Reagan wouldn't trade places with anyone in the world. He is in the very center of the country, and it almost seems as if he can hear the nation's heart beating.

How Hollywood Prepared Ronald Reagan for the World Stage: While working on *The Winning Team*, Reagan appreciates the value of hiring the best advisors. He also reinforces his belief in staying connected with the audience and speaking directly to them without a filter – essential lessons that contribute to his eventual designation as The Great Communicator.

Reagan displays his gift for dramatic acting in his portrayal of the troubled Grover Cleveland Alexander.
(Photo courtesy doctormacro.com)

A real Western at last!

(Author collection)

Chapter Fourteen
LAW AND ORDER

After fifteen years in Hollywood – and over thirty years since aspiring to be the next Tom Mix – Reagan has finally achieved his dream: He is about to star in a real Western. Sure, he appeared in *Santa Fe Trail* (1940) and *The Last Outpost* (1951) – two movies set in the West – but those stories were about the Army, not Western gunslingers. This is the first time he'll appear in the real thing.

He loves the title of the picture – *Law and Order* – because it's what he believes in. But he especially loves that he will play a U.S. marshal, someone with a badge, a gun, a horse, a ranch – everything he's always wanted in a picture.

Wyatt Earp (1848-1929), one of the old West's most legendary figures, was the inspiration for Frame Johnson, the main character in *Law and Order*.

The movie is based on the novel *Saint Johnson* by W.R. Burnett – a book Reagan admires for its story and style of telling. Reagan learns that Burnett was inspired to write the book after reading a biography of legendary U.S. Marshal Wyatt Earp and his infamous gunfight at the O.K. Corral.

Reagan hopes to make the story and its main character – U.S. Marshal Frame Johnson – his own. This is the third time the book has been adapted for the screen. A 1932 version starred Walter Huston and a 1940 version featured Johnny Mack Brown in the lead. While Reagan guesses he can hold his own against the latter, he figures he has a slim chance of measuring up to Huston – one of the best actors of all time and father of director John Huston.

During the summer of 1952, when Reagan reports to Universal for the costume fittings, it's the best kind of dress up – a real Western outfit, something he wants to wear all the time. As the tailor fits him for his costumes, Reagan keeps thinking back to his boyhood days in Dixon, when he loved to put on his cowboy hat and ride around on a broom pretending it was a horse.

But this is the real thing – he is one stylish looking cowboy, with fitted shirts and perfectly draped pants and kerchiefs tied at a jaunty angle. The costumers also fit him with a six-shooter and holster, with the gun positioned on his right side. But, try as he might, Reagan can't seem to get the doggone gun out of the holster.

Reagan rides high in the saddle. A reviewer writes of the film: "Ronald Reagan, in his first Western, indicates that he is more at home in a leather vest and ten-gallon hat than he ever was in a business suit."

How humiliating! For over a decade he's been begging to get into a Western, and now that he's in one he can't even do the basics.

Reagan goes off behind the Livery Stable on the backlot and tries to practice getting the gun out of the holster. But it's as if his hand won't obey his brain – he has never felt so clumsy.

"Need some help with that?" a voice with a slight twang calls out.

Reagan turns and sees Cliff Lyons, the stuntman for the movie – a Hollywood veteran renowned for his daring and skill.

"I feel like I'm all thumbs," Reagan says, flashing Lyons an embarrassed grin.

"Try it again, and let me watch," Lyons tells him.

Reagan does no better this time, fumbling with the revolver – and if it were loaded, he figures he would have shot himself in the foot.

After watching Reagan for a few seconds, Lyons starts to double over with laughter.

Portions of *Law and Order* were shot on the Western Street of the Universal backlot, the site of thousands of Western movies — including those starring Reagan's boyhood idol, Tom Mix.

(Photo: Corbis Images)

Reagan feels his face flush and not from the heat. He's both embarrassed and a little angry at Lyons' lack of sensitivity. While Reagan has a good sense of humor, this time he fails to see what's so funny. Finally, Lyons stops laughing and points to Reagan's holster.

"You're wearing your gun on the wrong side," he says.

"But I'm right-handed," Reagan explains.

"Not with a gun, you're not," Lyons adds.

Lyons trots off and comes back a minute later with a left-side holster, which Reagan threads onto his belt. When he draws, the gun slides out of the holster smooth and easy. He tries a few more times until he's sure. Yessiree, he's a left-handed gunslinger.

"How did you know?" Reagan asks the stunt man.

"Oh, I just figured you for one of those left-handers that the teachers changed to a right-hander in school."

CHAPTER FOURTEEN: LAW AND ORDER

Veteran Hollywood stuntman Cliff Lyons (above right, in a scene from the 1939 movie *Frontiers of '49*) began his career in the early 1920s. In *Law and Order*, he stages one of his most dangerous stunts of all time. He falls from a speeding buckboard directly into the path of a stagecoach drawn by four galloping horses.

Red Rock Canyon, California, the setting for the chase scenes in *Law and Order*.
(Photo: U.S. Department of Interior)

Reagan nods and says, "Thanks, Cliff. You saved me from a humiliating debut."

"Debut?" Lyons says.

"My first Western," Reagan tells him.

"And this one marks number one thousand for me," Lyons says, tips his hat, and ambles off.

The shoot begins the day after Labor Day. While most of the movie is slated for Universal's backlot in North Hollywood, the filming kicks off with a week's location shooting in Red Rock Canyon, near the Mojave Desert, about a hundred miles northeast of Los Angeles.

The landscape is breathtaking – and so rugged and rustic that Reagan can easily believe he is back in 1882, when the story is set. He is truly in his element – an active man in an action picture, at last.

First, they shoot a few scenes from the beginning of the movie, where Reagan's character, U.S. Marshall Frame Johnson, captures the Durango Kid, played by Wally Cassell. Then they shoot the end of the picture, when Frame goes after his black sheep brother Jimmy to make him face justice for murder. Jimmy, played by Universal contract player Russell Johnson, and Frame engage in a shootout on the cliffs. Jimmy – also a left-hander – shoots Frame, then feels instant remorse and brings him back to town, hoping to save his life.

"Don't come any closer, Frame. I'm warning you. I'll shoot. I mean it, Frame!" Jimmy Johnson (Russell Johnson) warns brother Frame Johnson (Ronald Reagan) in a final scene from *Law and Order*. Both actors are left-handed shooters.

From left, Alex Nicol, Russell Johnson, and Ronald Reagan play brothers in *Law and Order*. Both Nicol and Johnson go on to enjoy busy careers in movies and television – and Reagan eventually joins them in the then-new medium.
(Author collection)

Reagan enjoys the outdoor scenes and working on a horse. It makes him feel like a real cowboy. He can't help but notice that Russell Johnson seems uncomfortable on a horse and considers offering him a few pointers. But he thinks the better of it, not wanting to offend the fine young actor.

During breaks, the two men engage in friendly chats and Reagan learns that Johnson had one of the most dangerous jobs during WWII – as a bombardier. After flying forty-four combat missions, he was shot down in action in the Philippines – and received a Purple Heart and numerous other awards for valor.

After a week in Red Rock Canyon, the crew is back at the Universal backlot – where Reagan's childhood idol Tom Mix made so many movies. Reagan is glad that he's close to home. He finds it hard to be away from Nancy for even a few hours, let alone an entire week – especially since their first child is due soon.

Reagan has never been happier in his personal life – and he is hoping his professional life will take a permanent turn for the better, with more Westerns, action movies, and adventure films.

While he had high expectations for this movie, it isn't turning out the way he'd imagined. He doesn't like to criticize his fellow performers, but the acting is all over the map – with the cast getting no guidance from Nathan Juran, an Oscar-winning art director in only his second outing as director. Juran seems more interested in the technical aspects of the movie than in advising the cast members on their performances.

Dorothy Malone plays Reagan's love interest in *Law and Order* – and feels right at home making a Western, since she grew up in Dallas, Texas. Malone enjoys working with Reagan, calling him, "Positive and a lot of fun." In his autobiography, *Where's the Rest of Me?*, Reagan says the two best things about *Law and Order* were Technicolor and Dorothy Malone. In 1956, Malone wins an Oscar as best supporting actress for her performance in *Written on the Wind*.

(Author collection)

While the actors who play his brothers are delivering excellent work, as is Dorothy Malone as his love interest, many of the other players seem to be trying to upstage one another. As a result, the performances are too large for the roles, with little continuity. Reagan winces when he hears some of the actors deliver their lines. Everything seems to be said with at least a few exclamation points.

They're forming a lynch mob!!
They're coming to get Durango!!!
He's bluffing, boys, let's get him!!!!
Nobody's gonna take my gun!!!!!

Reagan is superstitious – which he chalks up to his Irish blood – and is somewhat put off by one aspect of the story: A mortician (Chubby Johnson) dogs his steps in the movie. The undertaker and his hearse follow Johnson and his brothers from Tombstone, where the story begins, to a remote part of Arizona, where Frame and family retire to a ranch. Reagan doesn't like to think about death – even when it's in a movie.

The picture is peopled with stock characters, including a corrupt sheriff, an upstanding judge, and a dance hall girl with a heart of gold. Despite the histrionics and clichéd performances from some of the actors, Reagan is determined that his performance and his character will be fleshed out – and that he'll be able to hold his head up when he sees himself on the screen. He wants his Western debut to be memorable.

"I give you my word I'll shoot the first man who starts for these steps." Reagan looks like a million bucks in his tailored Western garb, but looks can be deceiving. He has a major allergic reaction to his outfit – the one he'd been so enamored of just a short time before – made of moleskin, a type of heavy cotton fabric. Shooting is delayed while the star's hives heal and the costumers scramble to find a fabric that will match the clothing already shot.

The shoot days are long and so many things go wrong that the crew begins to murmur that the production is cursed. The villain in the movie (Preston Foster) misses the breakaway glass in the showdown with Frame Johnson and smashes through a real window – resulting in deep cuts to his back. Both Alex Nicol and Dennis Weaver sustain bruised stomachs when hit by misfiring blanks. Other mishaps include a horse stepping on Reagan's foot, powder burns to Alex Nicol's ear, and a twenty-pound lamp crashing down on the sheriff (Barry Kelley). When Reagan shoots his rifle, the blast sets off a bee swarm that threatens the crew and stops production. A prop man has to find the queen and lead the rest of the bees off the set.

The Family Johnson: Jimmy Johnson (played by Russell Johnson, left) assists a wounded Frame Johnson (Ronald Reagan, right). *Law and Order* also features actor Chubby Johnson. (Author collection.)

Dorothy Malone tries to lighten the mood by writing poems about her fellow actors. When Alex Nicol meets his demise in the film, she pens this rhyme for him:

The western star was laid to rest, upon a summer day.
His epitaph – now please don't laugh – had just this much to say:
"Point skyward when they ask you, pard – say, 'he went thataway.'"

The local judge (Richard Garrick) implores Frame Johnson to help rid the community of bad influences, saying: *"Mr. Johnson, this town is a sinkhole of violence and evil! We want a man who's big enough to oppose their organization!! We've decided you're that man!!!"* The future president tries to give an understated performance while a former president looks on.

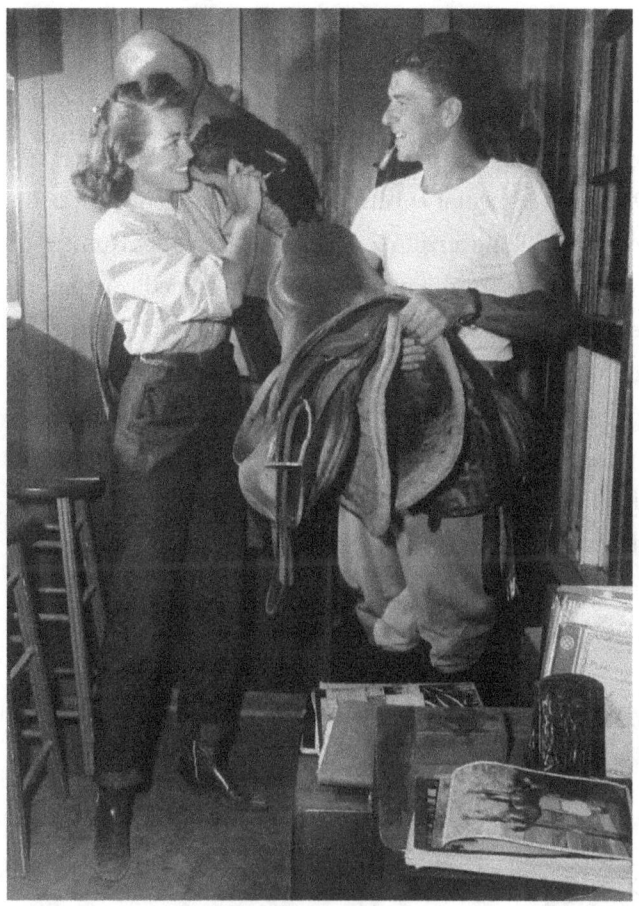

Costars Dorothy Malone and Ronald Reagan were both comfortable in Western attire – and in Westerns.
(Photo courtesy of Dorothy Malone)

Reagan, too, tries to keep everyone's spirits up – telling jokes, stories, and anecdotes between scenes. No one ever gets tired of the tale about how he finally managed to stand as tall as Errol Flynn.

A few weeks after the picture wraps, Reagan and Nancy are at a horse show when Nancy goes into labor. Daughter Patricia Ann Reagan – who later decides to be known by Davis, her mother's maiden name – is born on October 21, 1952. Since Patti almost made her entrance during a horse exhibition, Reagan figures she'll love growing up on the ranch.

While Reagan would still love to make a classic Western, he knows this is something over which he has no control. Anyway, he is living the Western – on his ranch, with his horses, his land, his fences – as star, director, producer, and rancher. And, best of all, he has the perfect woman to share it all with.

How Hollywood Prepared Ronald Reagan for the World Stage: Making *Law and Order* was a pivotal experience for Reagan. For over a decade, he had anticipated making a real Western. When the opportunity presented itself, it was not the ideal experience he'd imagined. But he made the best of the situation, and tried to see the bright side – at least he was outdoors riding a horse. Reagan was optimistic, yet realistic – he could dream big, yet accept a less-than-perfect outcome. In his political career, this translated to a willingness to negotiate and a desire to find common ground – qualities that led to his successful dealings with the Soviet Union on nuclear arms reduction.

From 1951-1966, Reagan and Nancy spend most weekends at their three-hundred acre ranch in Malibu Canyon.

(Reagan Family Photo, used by permission)

EVER AN OPTIMIST, REAGAN SMILES THROUGH GOOD TIMES AND BAD — BELIEVING, AS HIS MOTHER TOLD HIM, THAT EVERY CLOUD HAS A SILVER LINING.

(Photo: Reagan Library)

Chapter Fifteen

CATTLE QUEEN OF MONTANA

It's 1954 and Reagan and Nancy have been married for two years. But it's a challenge for Reagan to make enough money to take care of all his obligations. He's resisting taking the higher paying television roles, concerned that a move into the small screen will end his big-screen career. Still, he doesn't want to make just any movie. He's turned down a number of abysmal scripts – a decision that Nancy has fully supported – and while the time off is welcome, it just doesn't work financially. Yes, he has plenty to do in his life and stays constantly busy with the family, the ranch, and the horses, but he needs money to keep it all going.

Throughout Reagan's life, his mother has reiterated that everything works out for the best. This belief is now ingrained – and Reagan has faith that somehow he will get a good-paying assignment and these money worries will fade away.

And so it happens that his agent at Lew Wasserman's company, MCA, calls to say that he's been offered a lead role in *Cattle Queen of Montana* – an A picture starring Barbara Stanwyck. This sounds good to Reagan. He admires Stanwyck – and thinks it bodes well for his career to make a movie with one of the top stars in Hollywood.

"Send over the script," Reagan tells his agent, an amiable man named Art Park.

"It's a Western," Park replies, "you get to ride horses."

"I need to read the script," Reagan says.

He has an unpleasant flashback to *Law and Order*. Never again will he agree to do a movie just because it's a Western.

"Bogeaus says they're still working on the screenplay," Park replies, naming the movie's producer. "But he gave me the broad outlines of what it's about."

Park explains that the movie is set in the late 1800s, and tells the story of a lady rancher against the world in the wilds of Montana. He mentions that it's an RKO picture and Howard Hughes is putting up the money – trying to keep the studio solvent.

Reagan has always admired Stanwyck, but what sells him on the picture is its location: Glacier National Park in northwestern Montana near the Canadian border – someplace he's never visited.

So in late June 1954, Nancy, with not-yet-two-year-old Patti in tow, drops Reagan off at Union Station for the ride to Seattle, where he'll change for a Great Northern train that will take him right to the park. He hugs his girls tight and doesn't want to let them go. He knows it's going to be a long month away from home.

Union Station in downtown Los Angeles is a frequent launching point for Reagan during his movie career. He takes trains to and from locations, and feels more comfortable on the ground than in the air.
(Photo courtesy of University of Southern California, on behalf of the USC Special Collections.)

Aboard the train, Reagan runs into John Alton, the cinematographer for *Cattle Queen of Montana*. When they'd met recently at a social event, Reagan mentioned he was taking a nice, long, relaxing train to the location. Alton said that might be a good way for him to study the terrain before getting to the set.

As they enjoy the scenery – a straight shot north through some of California's most breathtaking country – Alton sketches and the two men talk about their lives, families, and careers. Alton explains that he comes from a small country – Hungary – and still finds it difficult to imagine the vastness of America. Reagan says that he comes from a large country, and still has trouble grasping the vastness of America.

CHAPTER FIFTEEN: CATTLE QUEEN OF MONTANA

In July 1954, Reagan and cinematographer John Alton take the Great Northern Empire Builder from Seattle, Washington, to Glacier National Park in Montana. The journey gives them time to appreciate the treasures of the American landscape.

(Great Northern publicity photo by Hedrich Blessing Studios, Great Northern Railway Historical Society collection.)

Reagan tells Alton about his disappointment that *Stallion Road* was shot in black and white – and the producers didn't take advantage of the movie's luxuriant setting: the Sierra Madre Mountains. He's happy *Cattle Queen* will be shot in color – so audiences around the world can appreciate one of America's crown jewels.

Then Reagan remembers something. He asks Alton: "Have you seen a script?"

"I only wish," Alton replies.

They change trains in Seattle, Washington, for the Great Northern Empire Builder, which travels right to the park. As they pile on the miles, Reagan has time to think about what's in store. The picture has the markings of a winning Western, starting with the man at the helm: Allan Dwan, one of Hollywood's most esteemed directors, who started his career in the silent era and went on to make many highly regarded films, including *Sands of Iwo Jima* (1949).

As the train digs deeper and deeper into the countryside, Reagan feels as if he's entered a new world, somewhere mysterious and magical. He has never been to this part of the country and is awestruck at its splendor and grandeur. He feels certain this is the place that inspired "purple mountains majesty." This is big sky country, with vast vistas and mountains that touch the heavens.

The train pulls into the station in East Glacier Park at around noon. A production assistant waits with a dolly to transport their belongings. Reagan and

When Reagan gets off the Great Northern train, he realizes he's just one of many people coming to enjoy the wonders of Glacier National Park. The location is a popular vacation spot for people across the country. When it opened as a national park in 1910, its advertising featured the slogan, "See America first" – to address East Coasters who spent vacations in Europe.

(Photo: National Park Service)

Alton follow the young man to a flatbed truck, where he ties down the luggage. Reagan and Alton squeeze into the front seat of the truck and enjoy the elevated views during the hour-long drive to the location.

When the driver lets them out at St. Mary Lodge, it's chillier than Reagan anticipated, and he hasn't brought any clothes for cool weather – after all, it's July. The thought crosses his mind that it's going to be a lot colder at night.

Reagan is anxious to get his hands on a script so he can start to prepare his role. He heads out to search for the director, who is already conferring with John Alton. Reagan finds the two men at the edge of St. Mary Lake discussing a scene. After introducing himself to Dwan and shaking hands, Reagan puts in his request for a script.

Dwan, a lively man around seventy years old, leans forward on his cane, tips back his cowboy hat, and says, "Don't worry so much, Ron."

Then Dwan raises his cane and points at the surroundings – the mountains, the lake, the trees, the sky, the clouds.

"Enjoy yourself," he says.

Reagan smiles and nods, then makes his way back to the lodge. He is starting to feel nervous. He prides himself on always coming to the set prepared, but how can he prepare if he doesn't have a script?

He figures he'll follow Dwan's advice and go out and enjoy himself. Problem is, as he'd read in his guidebook on the train, Glacier National Park is one million acres. Where does he begin to explore?

When he gets back to the lodge, he finds the proprietor, Hugh Black, a tall, lanky man with a crew cut and glasses. Reagan asks Black if anyone can give him a brief tour.

Black says the only available person is his twelve-year-old son Roscoe.

"Great," Reagan says. "When can we go?"

"As soon as he's done with his work," Black tells him.

"What kind of work?" Reagan asks.

"He has to finish cleaning the bathrooms and changing the towels."

Reagan is eager to start enjoying the great outdoors. He decides to search out Roscoe and see how far along he is with his chores.

He finds the boy in the bathroom of one of the guest rooms scrubbing the toilet with a brush. After introducing himself and explaining why he's there, Reagan asks Roscoe when he thinks he'll be done with his work.

While making *Cattle Queen of Montana,* Reagan stays at St. Mary Lodge, near St. Mary Lake (pictured here). Reagan is awestruck by the beautiful surroundings, and especially enjoys gazing at the luxuriant clouds and their reflections in the water.

(Photo: Chris Peterson)

"Not for at least another hour," Roscoe says.

"How about if I lend you a hand?" Reagan asks. "Then we can get out of here faster."

Soon, Reagan is in the bathroom next door scrubbing the basin and tub, cleaning the toilet, mopping the floor, and putting out fresh towels. He repeats the scene a few more times before Roscoe tells him they're finished.

When they get outside, Roscoe pops into a shed and finds two fishing rods and a tackle box.

"Best fishing in the world up here," he says to Reagan.

On their stroll toward St. Mary Lake, Reagan tells the boy about his days as a lifeguard on the Rock River near his home in Dixon, Illinois.

"Did you ever save anybody?" Roscoe asks.

"A few," Reagan tells him.

"How many?"

"A lucky seventy-seven," Reagan reveals.

As they stroll along, Reagan knows his jaw is hanging open – but he can't help it. He finds it hard to take in everything. He feels so small – like a paper cutout in a museum diorama. This is all too perfect to be real. He is mesmerized looking at the pristine aqua lake with the shadows of clouds dancing over it. The clouds, too, are fascinating. Living in Los Angeles, he's become used to living without clouds – but here they are, the kind of clouds he remembers from his childhood in Illinois: Big, fat, round, and full of promise. Clouds were the symbol his mother always used when she delivered her look-for-the-silver-lining talks.

Reagan feels nearly hypnotized by all the beauty surrounding him. But he doesn't want to be rude, so he asks Roscoe about himself and his family. He learns that Roscoe's parents opened the lodge about twenty years before. The family lives in Minnesota most of the year, and runs the lodge during the summer months.

"Do you ever get used to all this?" Reagan asks, indicating the surroundings.

Roscoe shakes his head "no."

Reagan smiles and pats Roscoe on the back saying, "That's the way it should be."

As they fish, Reagan and Roscoe talk about something they're both interested in – sports, mainly baseball and football. Reagan shares a few tales about his years as an announcer for the Cubs, and offers a few anecdotes about making *Knute Rockne: All American*.

An encounter with a grizzly bear in Glacier National Park cuts short Reagan's fishing expedition at St. Mary Lake.
(Photo: Chris Peterson)

Just then, Reagan turns and sees what looks like a ten-story-high grizzly bear. Roscoe whispers for him to drop the fishing rod and start walking. Reagan notices that Roscoe looks a lot paler all of a sudden. He wonders why. After all, they wouldn't allow a dangerous grizzly in a public park, would they? This bear must be tame, mustn't it?

Roscoe whispers that they'll probably be okay if the mother bear doesn't have a cub around. Reagan doesn't like the sound of the word "probably." They start to walk faster.

"What do we do if she comes after us?" he asks.

Roscoe says he's heard that you should run downhill. Reagan doesn't like the sound of "heard" – as if no one has lived to tell about it.

"Why's that?" Reagan whispers.

Roscoe says he's *heard* (that word again!) that bears are too top-heavy to run downhill. What follows is what feels like an endless walk, stiff legged, fast, and frightening, not knowing if the bear is following close behind.

When they finally make it back to the lodge, Reagan feels as if he has escaped a disaster. He thanks Roscoe for the fishing trip and the tour, and then returns to the haven of his room and flops on his bed. What if something had happened to him? He wouldn't have made it home to his mama bear and baby bear. That was an eventuality too terrible to even ponder.

When the sun goes down at almost ten o'clock, Reagan feels a deep longing for his girls back home. He has to turn away from the magnificent pink and purple clouds above the mountains and lake. The crushing beauty makes him feel lonelier with each passing minute. He wishes Nancy were here to share this – the silhouettes of the trees, the jewel-like clouds, the glass-still lake, the birds chirping their last notes day's end.

He has never felt such a deep, bone-wrenching loneliness. He gazes at the snow-covered peaks and the glaciers in the distance. He feels a breeze that goes right through him. It swirls around his head and seems to whisper secrets as old as time. All these things stir up longing in his soul, a longing to be home with the woman he loves. But how can he express to her with mere words how much he loves and misses her?

Reagan gets little sleep that night. Throughout the wee hours, he hears trucks barreling up to the lodge – his Hollywood compatriots bringing up the gear. Reagan tosses and turns and thinks about Nancy and Patti, hoping they're safe and well back home.

The next morning, he has an idea about how to give Nancy an inkling of how he's feeling. He'll write the letter to Patti and talk about his loneliness in a way that is simple, direct.

He writes a long letter about how he felt looking at the evening sky – addressing the letter to twenty-one-month-old Patti. He closes by writing: *"I'm counting on you to take care of Mommie and keep her safe for me because there wouldn't be any moon or stars in the sky without her. The breeze would whisper no secrets and the warmth would go out of the sun."*

The next morning, he finds a script shoved under his door with a note that says: Nine a.m. call time. He reads the script before going down to breakfast, and sees holes the size of meteors in the story.

He considers the material as he showers and shaves. The script is a mess, but he tries to focus on his role – and come up with ideas for improving the part. As he spreads shaving cream on his face and looks at himself in the mirror, he thinks about his more than fifteen years in movies – and never once has he played a bad guy. During more than half of *Cattle Queen of Montana*, the audience will think he's a black-hearted bum – instead of an undercover government agent, which he turns out to be.

Lake McDonald in Glacier National Park, Montana, as photographed by Ansel Adams in 1942. Reagan is excited about making *Cattle Queen of Montana* because it allows him to spend time in this pristine location, a place he's never before visited.

(Photo: National Park Service)

A highly accomplished horsewoman with a love of physical exertion, Barbara Stanwyck does her own riding and stunts in *Cattle Queen of Montana*, earning the respect of the Blackfeet Indians working on the picture.
(Author collection)

As he shaves, Reagan realizes how to fix the problem. Insert a scene between the agent and his boss at the beginning of the movie. This way, the audience will know the score – and the drama will rest in whether the evil rancher discovers his real identity. Yes, this would work – and it would make the picture a whole lot more entertaining.

He heads down to breakfast around seven and finds Miss Stanwyck nibbling on dry toast and flipping thought the script. When Missy – as her friends call her – sees Reagan, she stands and they engage in a warm hug. This is the first time he's worked with Stanwyck, but he knows her reputation: a total professional on-set and off. Among her colleagues, she is by far the most popular actress in Hollywood.

"How's Nancy?" Stanwyck asks. The two women appeared in *East Side, West Side* (1949) – one of Nancy's first movies after coming to Hollywood.

"Great," Reagan says. "The greatest."

After a bit more chitchat, they exchange a few words about the movie, the location, and the men at the helm – director Allan Dwan and producer Benedict Bogeaus.

"Allan is a love," Stanwyck gushes. "I like him almost as much as I like Capra – and I adore Capra."

"I hope he does something about the script," Reagan says aiming a finger like a six-shooter at his copy on the table.

"What can you expect from these kinds of pictures?" Stanwyck replies.

"Well, at least I get to ride a horse," Reagan tells her. "And they should have some good horseflesh up in these parts."

For his morning meal, Reagan orders something heartier than Stanwyck's slight breakfast – eggs, bacon, toast, pancakes, and oatmeal. He figures he'll work it all off before lunch.

Stanwyck is cordial, sitting with Reagan while he finishes his meal. But as soon as he downs the last bite, she gets up and excuses herself.

While Stanwyck goes off to have her hair and makeup attended to, Reagan heads out about an hour before call time to see how things are shaping up on the set. He feels winded just walking along. The location is at least a mile high – and that's in the valley, not the mountains.

He approaches an open area between the lake and the mountains. There, technicians scramble to unload trucks, while other crewmembers rush around shouting orders. The mood is tense – people racing around with little or no purpose – and the general impression is total chaos.

He sees Allan Dwan huffing up the path and decides to have a chat with him about the script. He pulls him aside and offers a few suggestions, but Dwan shrugs him off, saying, "Not now, Ron."

As Dwan walks away, leaning heavily on his cane, Reagan says, "Is it all right if I spend the day in the saddle?"

Allan Dwan (1885-1981) started to direct films during the silent era and enjoyed an active career through the 1960s. While making *Cattle Queen of Montana,* Dwan and his producing partner had many disagreements about the script.

Dwan doesn't even turn around. "If the scene calls for it, you can ride," he says. "We start shooting at nine."

Reagan follows after Dwan, calling, "Allan!" But he has to stop to catch his breath. They are so high up that he can't walk and talk at the same time.

Viewing the turmoil on the set, Reagan would lay odds that Dwan's prediction will not come true. Reagan doubts that they'll get any shooting done at all on this day.

This is the first picture Reagan has made since television became a dominant force in the industry. He's heard that the new medium is luring away all the best talent with steady work and hefty paychecks. Judging by this crew, the rumors seem to be true. This is a ragtag bunch that looks overwhelmed and overwrought. It seems as if the producer had just rounded up whatever stragglers he could locate and hired them for the picture.

Reagan moseys toward the horse corral. As he approaches, he sees there are two distinct sections and wonders why the horses have been separated. While he studies the horses, he notices that one corral contains fine-looking thoroughbreds, and the other seems like a playground for ponies. On closer look, he sees that these aren't ponies or even yearlings – they're what look like full-grown runts. He shakes his head – realizing he's never seen horses this small before. He wonders why they're here and who's going to ride these hobbyhorses.

Reagan spots what he figures are local ranchers milling around one of the cabins. He heads over and introduces himself, but they are men of few words – and, try as he might, Reagan can't draw them out. This is one tough crowd.

He makes his way to where the crew is congregated and finds Allan Dwan and producer Ben Bogeaus in a heated argument. Good old Allan is actually pitching Reagan's idea to Bogeaus. Reagan smiles – and here he thought Dwan had tossed away his suggestion.

"The script is solid!" yells Bogeaus, who's known in Hollywood as a director of B-minus movies.

After a few more heated exchanges, Dwan throws up his hands in surrender.

The first scene calls for Stanwyck to bathe in St. Mary River. She is supposed to have just come in from a long journey herding her cattle from Texas to Montana. The air temperature is cool – around fifty – and, according to an assistant director, the water temperature is downright freezing.

Dwan suggests a double for the long shots, but Stanwyck won't hear of it. She submits to take after take in the frigid water without uttering a complaint.

After what seems like hours shooting Stanwyck's brief bathing scene, it's time to move on.

Dwan goes over Reagan's part with him. He'll ride up as Stanwyck is getting dressed behind a boulder. Great, Reagan thinks. He can finally do what he loves to do – play with horses. To Reagan, work never really seems like work if he's outdoors riding a horse.

As Reagan is studying the script, he feels someone place a horse's reins into his hand. He smiles, but when he looks at his mount, the happy expression falls from his face.

It's one of the scrawny goats from the corral! There is no way he is going to ride this ridiculous-looking pipsqueak.

Reagan guides the little beast over to the corral and leads him inside, then sizes up the thoroughbreds and decides on one. He has no fears about his ability to handle any horse. Why should he? He's been working with horses on virtually a daily basis for over twenty years.

"What d'ya think yer doin'?" a gruff voice calls out.

Reagan turns and sees one of the local ranchers striding toward him.

"I need a horse for the next scene," Reagan explains, leading a tall, black stallion out of the corral.

"Put him back," the rancher says.

The assistant director runs up and gets between Reagan and the rancher.

"Sorry for the misunderstanding," the assistant director says to the rancher. Then he turns to Reagan and says, "That one is for you." He points to the short, skinny horse Reagan just led back to the corral.

"I hope you're kidding," Reagan says.

While the rancher stares hot pokers at Reagan, the assistant director pulls him aside.

"Sorry, Mr. Reagan, but that's the way it is."

"But who's riding the good horses?"

The assistant director nods toward the locals milling around the cabin.

"They are."

Before Reagan can ask any more questions, the assistant director says that the locals are playing members of the posse in the movie. The ranchers are supplying

Reagan writes Nancy about the "scrawny goat" he has to ride in *Cattle Queen of Montana,* saying it's about the size of the yearlings on their ranch. In this scene from the trailer, Reagan seems to wear an embarrassed grin while riding the pint-sized palomino.

the horses and insist on riding the best mounts. They don't want any Hollywood rubes messing with their prized possessions.

"But I'm an experienced rider," Reagan says. "I was in the Cavalry for seven years!"

"They said we can take it or leave it," the assistant director tells him. "Sorry. If we don't go along with it, they've threatened to take all their horses and hit the trail."

Another assistant rushes up and says, "Hurry, Mr. Reagan. They're calling for you."

Reagan strides over to the corral and retrieves his tiny companion. He feels kind of sorry for Pee Wee. He realizes it's not the little guy's fault that he's so small. But, still, Reagan knows he's going to look ridiculous sitting on this toy horse. It seems that whenever he gets his hopes up about making a Western, something totally unexpected happens. After all, the least you could expect when making a Western is to get a normal-sized horse. He realizes that the horses and the crew have a lot in common.

He leads Pee Wee to the location, opting not to ride him unless absolutely necessary. It would seem almost criminal to subject the tike to his nearly two hundred pounds. After Reagan gets to the assigned spot near the shore, he hops on his little friend.

When the assistant yells, "Quiet on the set," his tone is plaintive and pleading – as if he's given up all hope of anything going right on this picture.

All Reagan can think about is finishing with some grace and dignity and getting back to Nancy and Patti. The next morning, he gets up early and writes a letter.

> *Tuesday, July 13, 1954*
> *Last night was another one of those nights – just too beautiful to stand. So tonight I'll probably be looking at the Moon which means I'll be looking at you – literally and figuratively because it lays far to the South of this mountain top and that's where you are…I just see you in all the beauty there is because in you I've found all the beauty in my life.*

And so the days drag on. The first week feels like a year. A highlight, though, is working with the great Indian quick-draw artist, Rodd Redwing – an expert marksman whose claim to fame is drawing and firing his gun in two-tenths of a second. Redwing has coached many Hollywood stars, including Burt Lancaster, Anthony Quinn, and Charlton Heston.

Between takes Reagan welcomes Redwing's coaching. He tells the chief – a full-blooded Chickasaw – about how he discovered he was a left-handed shooter during the making of *Law and Order*. Redwing laughs, telling Reagan that he's lucky he figured it out.

Cattle Queen of Montana features Rodd Redwing (1904-1971), a Native American actor from the Chickasaw tribe, who started his career in 1931, appearing in Cecil B. DeMille's *Squaw Man*. During four decades in Hollywood, Redwing is also in demand as a coach – teaching would-be cowboys how to handle guns, tomahawks, knives, and whips. Redwing is pictured here in a scene from *Riders of the Pony Express*.
(Photo: Ken Jones Collection)

As the days eke by in dribs and drabs, it seems like forever that he's been away from home, Reagan thinks about the slow movement of time. He gazes up at the glaciers and the mountains, and feels a sense of awe at what nature has achieved. What matter these petty problems in a bit of lightweight entertainment? This magnificent place, the crown of the world, as the Blackfeet call it, strikes him dumb with wonder.

July 17, 1954

I'm lonesome and miss you both until it hurts...I love you so very much and miss you every minute. Be very careful of you.

Reagan is impressed working with the Blackfeet Indians, whose reservation is nearby. Many Indians have been cast in the movie, mainly in non-speaking roles. He learns that the chief is particularly impressed with Barbara Stanwyck and admires the way she rides and how she does all of her own stunts and difficult scenes, particularly bathing in the cold pond. The Blackfeet make Stanwyck an adopted member of their tribe and christen her Princess Many Victories.

The Blackfeet Indian Reservation is adjacent to Glacier National Park. Members of the Blackfeet Nation appear in *Cattle Queen of Montana*.
(Photo: George A. Grant, National Park Service)

Reagan appreciates working with Stanwyck, whom he calls "a great actress and a real pro."
(Photo: Mel Ruder/*Hungry Horse News*)

A month away from home seems like a century. In his bones, Reagan senses how glaciers form slowly over time. On the last day of shooting, he tries to take in his surroundings and remember everything just the way it is, mainly so he can describe it to Nancy. It might be nice to have a ranch up this way. As Stanwyck's character, Sierra Nevada Jones, says in the movie, "Montana grass is the best in the world."

He stops to take in the grandeur of the cliffs and the glaciers, the nobility of the peaks. He thinks about where he stands, right on the continental divide, the place where the waters part and flow in opposite directions, to the Pacific and the Atlantic. It is an awe-inspiring place to contemplate. He feels so proud and grateful to live in such a magnificent country. He realizes his whole life has been blessed. And, most blessed of all, he has Nancy to return to, and he knows she will be waiting for him with open arms.

Reagan performs while his train companion, John Alton (in white hat, at left), shoots the action. The actor feels confident that the cinematographer – an Oscar winner – will capture the magnificence of Glacier National Park on film. In this scene close to the end of the movie, Reagan blows up a supply of stolen munitions – accomplishing his mission as an undercover government agent.

(Photo: Mel Ruder/*Hungry Horse News*)

HOW HOLLYWOOD PREPARED RONALD REAGAN FOR THE WORLD STAGE: Making *Cattle Queen of Montana* put Reagan in touch with America the Beautiful – and allowed him to enjoy a month-long period where he experienced a profound emotional connection to the land. This deep love of country eventually propelled him into a political career – and kept him grounded throughout his years in government.

After a month in Montana, Reagan is happy to return to Nancy and little Patti – and glad when he can shoot the remainder of *Cattle Queen of Montana* close to home at the Iverson Movie Ranch in Chatsworth, California.

(Author collection)

Added Attraction

Tennessee's Partner

The following year, 1955, Reagan shoots another Western for the team of Bogeaus and Dwan. This one is called *Tennessee's Partner*, and he stars as Cowpoke, a miner turned gunslinger who meets a tragic end. The movie also re-teams him with one of his favorite costars, Rhonda Fleming. In the movie, Reagan plays a naïve innocent hoodwinked by a gold-digger played by Coleen Gray. But the truth comes out in the end.

John Payne stars as Tennessee opposite Ronald Reagan as Cowpoke in *Tennessee's Partner*, a 1955 movie loosely based on a Bret Harte story. In this still, Tennessee offers Cowpoke a cigarette – though Reagan neither smoked in the movie nor in real life. Many of the actors from *Cattle Queen of Montana* appear in *Tennessee's Partner* – with the same two men at the helm: Allan Dwan (director) and Benedict Bogeaus (producer).

(Author collection)

Fortunately, life is not imitating art. His real-life wife is as true blue as they come, and has married him for better or worse. They are going through some rough times financially – not enough good film roles to go around these days, ever since television arrived in the late 1940s. Despite his reluctance to appear on the "tube," Reagan soon finds his way onto the small screen in a big way – as host of *General Electric Theater*.

The G.E. assignment turns into an eight-year bonanza of work that finally brings Reagan and his family financial stability – and in many ways sets the stage for his career in politics. He spends months of each year on the road giving speeches and interacting with employees at General Electric plants. This allows him to not only hone his skills as a communicator, but also connect on a meaningful level to his fellow Americans.

Coleen Gray plays a villainess named Goldie who dupes Reagan's character, Cowpoke, in *Tennessee's Partner*. In real life, Gray was a friend of Reagan and Nancy – and they even attended the same church. Gray remembers Reagan as, "Fun, charming, and great to work with."

Post Script
HELLCATS OF THE NAVY

In 1957, Ronald Reagan and Nancy Davis appear in their first — and only — picture together: *Hellcats of the Navy*, a submarine adventure set during WWII. Reagan will go on to make only one more feature film — *The Killers* (1964) — while Nancy retires from movies after *Hellcats*. Reagan also enjoys a successful career in television, as host of *G.E. Theater* (1954-1962) and *Death Valley Days* (1964-1965), and guest star on many programs.

(Author collection)

"The movies, from the beginning, were a pure American enterprise in the tradition of private thought and execution. More than any other industry, its founders worked with raw materials that had no other market than people's emotions."

RONALD REAGAN
Where's the Rest of Me?

RONALD REAGAN was born in Tampico, Illinois, on February 6, 1911. After a successful career as a sports announcer, Warner Brothers Studio offered him a contract to star in movies. During his nearly thirty-year career as an actor, Reagan made fifty-three films – delivering tour de force performances as George Gipp in *Knute Rockne: All American,* and as Drake McHugh in *Kings Row.* From 1942-1945, Reagan served in the U.S. Cavalry Reserves and the U.S. Army Air Corps, where he earned the rank of Captain. While in the Army Air Corps, Reagan appeared in and narrated instructional and motivational films for the troops and the general public. When the war ended, Reagan resumed his acting career, and from 1947-1952 and again in 1959 served as president of the Screen Actors Guild. Reagan entered politics in 1966, when he was elected governor of California, serving two terms. In 1980, he was elected president of the United States, and again elected in 1984. His legacy includes influencing the fall of Communism and halting the nuclear arms race. Reagan passed away in 2004, at age ninety-three, after a long battle with Alzheimer's disease. He is buried at the Reagan Library in Simi Valley, California, which is also a repository of his papers and artifacts.

Films of Ronald Reagan

From 1937-1964, Ronald Reagan made fifty-three movies.
(Photo courtesy doctormacro.com)

Hellcats of the Navy, 1957.
(Author collection)

1. *Accidents Will Happen*, 1938
2. *An Angel From Texas*, 1940
3. *Angels Wash Their Faces*, 1939
4. *The Bad Man*, 1941
5. *Bedtime for Bonzo*, 1951
6. *Boy Meets Girl*, 1938
7. *Brother Rat*, 1938
8. *Brother Rat and a Baby*, 1940
9. *Cattle Queen of Montana*, 1954
10. *Code of the Secret Service*, 1939
11. *Cowboy From Brooklyn*, 1938
12. *Dark Victory*, 1939
13. *Desperate Journey*, 1942
14. *The Girl from Jones Beach*, 1949
15. *Girls on Probation*, 1938
16. *Going Places*, 1938
17. *The Hasty Heart*, 1950
18. *Hellcats of the Navy*, 1957
19. *Hell's Kitchen*, 1939
20. *Hollywood Hotel*, 1938
21. *Hong Kong*, 1952
22. *International Squadron*, 1941
23. *It's a Great Feeling*, 1949
24. *John Loves Mary*, 1949
25. *Juke Girl*, 1942
26. *The Killers*, 1964
27. *Kings Row*, 1942
28. *Knute Rockne: All American*, 1940
29. *The Last Outpost*, 1951
30. *Law and Order*, 1953
31. *Louisa*, 1950
32. *Love Is on the Air*, 1937
33. *Million Dollar Baby*, 1941
34. *Murder in the Air*, 1940
35. *Naughty But Nice*, 1939
36. *Night Unto Night*, 1949
37. *Nine Lives Are Not Enough*, 1941
38. *Prisoner of War*, 1954
39. *Santa Fe Trail*, 1940
40. *Secret Service of the Air*, 1939
41. *Sergeant Murphy*, 1938
42. *She's Working Her Way Through College*, 1952
43. *Smashing the Money Ring*, 1939
44. *Stallion Road*, 1947
45. *Storm Warning*, 1951
46. *Swing Your Lady*, 1938
47. *Tennessee's Partner*, 1955
48. *That Hagen Girl*, 1947
49. *This Is the Army*, 1943
50. *Tropic Zone*, 1953
51. *Tugboat Annie Sails Again*, 1940
52. *The Voice of the Turtle*, 1947
53. *The Winning Team*, 1952

RONALD REAGAN'S RESIDENCES 1937-1957

Biltmore Hotel
506 S. Grand Avenue, Los Angeles
Early June 1937

Plaza Hotel
1637 Vine Street, Hollywood
Mid-June 1937

Montecito Apartments
6650 Franklin Avenue, Hollywood
Late-June 1937 - Late 1938

1128 Cory Avenue, Hollywood
Late 1938 - Spring 1939

1326 Londonderry, Hollywood
Spring 1939 - Late 1941

9137 Cordell Drive, Los Angeles
Summer/Fall 1941 - Summer 1948

Eight-acre ranch, Northridge
1945 - 1951

1326 Londonderry, Hollywood
Summer 1948 - July 1952

Yearling Row Ranch, 300 acres, Malibu
March 1951 - 1966

941-½ Hilgard Avenue, Westwood
March 1952 - July 1952

1258 Amalfi Drive, Pacific Palisades
July 1952 - 1957

BIBLIOGRAPHY

BOOKS

Adler, Bill and Adler, Bill, Jr. *The Reagan Wit: The Humor of the American President.* New York: William Morrow and Company, Inc., 1998.

Alton, John. *Painting with Light.* Berkeley: University of California Press, 1995.

Anderson, Martin and Anderson, Annelise. *Reagan's Secret War: The Untold Story of His Fight to Save the World from Nuclear Disaster.* New York: Crown, 2009.

Atkins, Irene Kahn. *David Butler Interviews.* Metuchen, NJ: Scarecrow Press, 1993.

Base, Ron. *"If the Other Guy Isn't Jack Nicholson, I've Got the Part": Hollywood Tales of Big Breaks, Bad Luck, and Box-Office Magic.* Chicago: Contemporary Books, 1994.

Basten, Fred. E. *Paradise By the Sea: Santa Monica Bay: A Pictorial History of Santa Monica, Venice, Marina Del Rey, Ocean Park, Pacific Palisades, Topanga & Malibu.* Santa Monica, California: Hennessey & Ingalls, 2000.

Baumlin, James S. ed. *The Gillioz "Theatre Beautiful": Remembering Springfield's Theatre History, 1926-2006.* Springfield, Missouri: Moon City Press, 2006.

Benson, Harry. *The President & Mrs. Reagan: An American Love Story.* New York: Harry N. Abrams, Inc., 2003.

Boller, Paul F., Jr., and Davis, Ronald L. *Hollywood Anecdotes.* New York: Ballantine Books, 1987.

Borland, Jay and Vance, Malcolm. *The Ronald Reagan Hollywood Quiz Book.* New York: David M. Cohn Publishing, Inc., 1981.

Boyer, Mary Schmitt. *Indians Essential: Everything You Need to Know to Be a Real Fan!* Chicago: Triumph Books, 2007.

Brinkley, Douglas. *The Boys of Pointe Du Hoc: Ronald Reagan, D-Day, and the U.S. Army 2nd Ranger Battalion.* New York: William Morrow, 2005.

Brownstein, Ronald. *The Power and the Glitter: The Hollywood-Washington Connection.* New York: Pantheon Books, 1990.

Bruck, Connie. *When Hollywood Had a King: The Reign of Lew Wasserman, Who Leveraged Talent into Power and Influence.* New York: Random House, 2003.

Burnett, W.R. *Saint Johnson.* New York: The Dial Press, 1930.

Cannon, Lou. *President Reagan: The Role of a Lifetime.* New York: Public Affairs, 1991, 2000.

Cannon, Lou. *Governor Reagan: His Rise to Power.* New York: Public Affairs, 2003.

Cannon, Lou. *The Presidential Portfolio: A History Illustrated from the Collections of the Ronald Reagan Library and Museum.* New York: Public Affairs, 2001.

Carroll, Brendan G. *The Last Prodigy: A Biography of Erich Wolfgang Korngold.* Portland, Oregon: Amadeus Press, 1997.

Chafe, William H. *Private Lives/Public Consequences: Personality and Politics in Modern America.* Cambridge, MA: Harvard University Press, 2005.

Colacello, Bob. *Ronnie & Nancy: Their Path to the White House – 1911-1980.* New York: Warner Books, 2004.

Combs, James E. *Polpop: Politics and Popular Culture in America.* Madison, WI: Popular Press, 1984.

Davis, Patti. *The Way I See It: An Autobiography.* New York: G.P. Putnam's Sons, 1992.

Davis, Ronald L. *Zachary Scott: Hollywood's Sophisticated Cad.* Jackson, Mississippi: University of Mississippi Press, 2006.

Diggins, John Patrick. *Ronald Reagan: Fate, Freedom, and the Making of History.* New York: W.W. Norton & Company, 2007.

Djuff, Ray and Morrison, Chris. *Waterton and Glacier in a Snap! Fast Facts and Titillating Trivia.* Calgary: Rocky Mountain Books, 2005.

Edwards, Anne. *The Reagans: Portrait of a Marriage.* New York: St. Martin's Press, 2003.

Edwards, Anne. *Early Reagan: The Rise to Power.* New York: William Morrow and Company, Inc., 1987.

Eliot, Marc. *Reagan: The Hollywood Years.* New York: Harmony Books, 2008.

Ephron, Henry. *We Thought We Could Do Anything.* New York: W.W. Norton & Company, 1977.

Evans, Thomas W. *The Education of Ronald Reagan: The General Electric Years and the Untold Story of His Conversion to Conservatism.* New York: Columbia University Press, 2006,

Eubanks, Steve. *Quotable Reagan: Words of Wit, Wisdom, & Statesmanship by and About Ronald Reagan, America's Great Communicator.* Nashville, TN: TowleHouse Publishing, 2001.

Faulkner, William. *Stallion Road, a Screenplay.* Jackson, MS: University Press of Mississippi, 1989.

Flynn, Errol. *My Wicked, Wicked Ways.* New York: Cooper Square Press, 2003.

Freedland, Michael. *The Warner Brothers.* New York: St. Martin's Press, 1983.

Gardner, Gerald. *The Censorship Papers: Movie Censorship Letters from the Hays Office 1934 to 1968.* New York: Dodd, Mead & Company, 1987.

Goodwin, Betty. *Chasen's: Where Hollywood Dined.* Santa Monica, CA: Angel City Press, 1996.

Hatheway, Roger G. and Keller, Russell L. *Lake Arrowhead: Postcard History Series.* San Francisco: Arcadia Publishing Co., 2006.

Hayward, Steven F. *Greatness: Reagan, Churchill & the Making of Extraordinary Leaders.* New York: Crown Forum, 2005.

Higham, Charles. *Sisters: The Story of Olivia de Havilland & Joan Fontaine.* New York: Coward-McCann, Inc., 1984.

Hotchner, A.E. *Doris Day: Her Own Story.* New York: William Morrow and Company, Inc., 1975.

Humes, James C. *The Wit & Wisdom of Ronald Reagan.* Washington, DC: Regnery Publishing, Inc., 2007.

Huston, John. *An Open Book.* New York: Knopf, 1980.

Inge, M. Thomas ed. *Conversations with William Faulkner.* Jackson, Mississippi: University of Mississippi Press, 1999.

Kempton, Murray. *Rebellions, Perversities, and Main Events.* New York: Random House, 1994.

Knott, Stephen F. and Chidester, Jeffrey L. *At Reagan's Side: Insiders' Recollections from Sacramento to the White House.* Lanham, Maryland: Rowman & Littlefield Publishers, Inc., 2009.

Lawrence, Tom. *Pictures, a Park & a Pulitzer: Mel Ruder and the Hungry Horse News.* Helena: Farcountry Press, 2000.

Lomax, Becky. *Glacier National Park.* Emeryville, California: Avalon Travel Publishing, 2006.

McClelland, Doug. *Hollywood on Ronald Reagan: Friends and Enemies Discuss Our President, the Actor.* Winchester, MA: Faber and Faber, Inc., 1983.

McGivern, C. and Landesman, Fred. *Ronald Reagan: The Hollywood Years.* Great Britain: 4edge Ltd., 2004.

Mayer, Jane and McManus, Doyle. *Landslide: The Unmaking of the President 1984-1988.* Boston: Houghton Mifflin Company, 1988.

Minter, David L. *William Faulkner: His Life and Work.* Baltimore: Johns Hopkins University Press, 1997.

Morella, Joe and Epstein, Edward Z. *Jane Wyman: A Biography*. New York: Delacorte Press, 1985.

Neal, Patricia with DeNeut, Richard. *As I Am: An Autobiography*. New York: Simon and Schuster, 1988.

Noonan, Peggy. *When Character Was King: A Story of Ronald Reagan*. New York: Viking, 2001.

O'Brien, Pat. *The Wind at My Back: The Life and Times of Pat O'Brien*. Garden City, New York: 1964.

Pournelle, Jerry and Ing, Dean. *Mutual Assured Survival: Based on the Citizens Advisory Council's Report to the President*. New York: Simon and Schuster, 1984.

Price, Brick. *The Model Shipbuilding Handbook*. Radnor, Pennsylvania: Chilton Book Company, 1983.

Prindle, David F. *The Politics of Glamour: Ideology and Democracy in the Screen Actors Guild*. Madison, WI: The University of Wisconsin Press, 1988.

Quirk, Lawrence J. *Jane Wyman: The Actress and the Woman*. New York: Dembner Books, 1986.

Reagan, Maureen. *First Father, First Daughter: A Memoir*. Boston: Little, Brown and Company, 1989.

Reagan, Michael with Denney, Jim. *In the Words of Ronald Reagan: The Wit, Wisdom, and Eternal Optimism of America's 40th President*. Nashville, TN: Nelson Books, 2004.

Reagan, Michael with Denney, Jim. *Twice Adopted*. Nashville, TN: Broadman & Holman Publishers, 2004.

Reagan, Michael with Hyams, Joe. *On the Outside Looking In*. New York: Zebra Books, 1988.

Reagan, Nancy with Libby, Bill. *Nancy*. New York: William Morrow and Company, Inc., 1980.

Reagan, Nancy with Novak, William. *My Turn: The Memoirs of Nancy Reagan*. New York: Random House, 1989.

Reagan, Nancy and Reagan, Ronald. *I Love You, Ronnie: The Letters of Ronald Reagan to Nancy Reagan*. New York: Random House, 2000.

Reagan, Ronald. *Where's the Rest of Me?* New York: Duell, Sloan and Pearce, 1965.

Reagan, Ronald. *An American Life: The Autobiography*. New York: Simon and Schuster, 1990.

Reagan, Ronald. *The Reagan Diaries*. New York: HarperCollins Publishers, 2007.

Ronald Reagan Presidential Foundation. *Ronald Reagan: An American Hero*. New York: Dorling Kindersley, 2001.

Schroeder, Alan. *Celebrity-in-Chief: How Show Business Took Over the White House*. Cambridge, Massachusetts: Westview Press, 2004.

Shannon, Mike. *Baseball: The Writer's Game*. Dulles, VA: Potomac Books, 2002.

Sharp, Kathleen. *Mr. & Mrs. Hollywood: Edie and Lew Wasserman and Their Entertainment Empire*. New York: Carroll & Graf Publishers, 2003.

Sherman, Robert G. *Quiet on the Set! Motion Picture History at the Iverson Movie Location Ranch*. Chatsworth, CA: Sherway Publishing Company, 1984.

Shirley, Craig. *Reagan's Revolution: The Untold Story of the Campaign that Started It All*. Nashville, TN: Nelson Current, 2005.

Siegel, Don. *A Siegel Film*. London: Faber and Faber, 1993.

Skinner, Kiron K., Anderson, Annelise, and Anderson, Martin, eds. *Stories in His Own Hand: The Everyday Wisdom of Ronald Reagan*. New York: The Free Press, 2001.

Skinner, Kiron K., Anderson, Annelise, and Anderson, Martin. *Reagan: A Life in Letters*. New York: Free Press, 2003.

Skipper, John C. *Wicked Curve: The Life and Troubled Times of Grover Cleveland Alexander*. Jefferson, NC: McFarland & Company, Inc., 2006.

Spada, James. *Ronald Reagan: His Life in Pictures*. New York: St. Martin's Press, 2000.

Speakes, Larry with Pack, Robert. *Speaking Out: Inside the Reagan White House*. New York: Charles Scribner's Sons, 1988.

Sperling, Cass Warner and Millner, Cork with Warner, Jr., Jack. *Hollywood Be Thy Name: The Warner Brothers Story*. Rocklin, California: Prima Publishing, 1994.

Temple Black, Shirley. *Child Star*. New York: McGraw-Hill Publishing Company, 1988.

Thomas, Bob. *Clown Prince of Hollywood: The Antic Life and Times of Jack L. Warner*. New York: McGraw-Hill Publishing Company, 1990.

Thomas, Tony. *The Films of Ronald Reagan*. Secaucus, NJ: Citadel Press, 1980.

Vaughn, Stephen. *Ronald Reagan in Hollywood: Movies and Politics*. Cambridge, England: Cambridge University Press, 1994.

Waldrup, Carole Chandler. *Wives of the American Presidents*, Second Edition. Jefferson, NC: McFarland & Company, Inc., 2006.

Wayne, Jane Ellen. *Stanwyck: The Star, the Success, the Survivor; The Untold Biography of the Woman*. New York: Arbor House, 1985.

Watterson, John Sayle. *The Games Presidents Play: Sports and the Presidency*. Baltimore: Johns Hopkins University Press, 2006.

Weller, Sheila. *Dancing at Ciro's*. New York: St. Martin's Press, 2003.

Wilkerson, Tichi and Borie, Marcia. *Hollywood Legends: The Golden Years of the Hollywood Reporter*. Los Angeles: Tale Weaver Publishing, 1988.

Williams, Dino and Williams, Alexa. *The Story of Hollywoodland*. Los Angeles: Papavasilopoulos Press, 1992.

Williams, Gregory Paul. *The Story of Hollywood: An Illustrated History*. Los Angeles: BL Press LLC, 2005.

Wright, P.M. *New Manual of Model Shipbuilding*. New York: D. Van Nostrand Company, Inc., 1962.

Yager, Edward M. *Ronald Reagan's Journey: Democrat to Republican*. Lanham, MD: Rowman & Littlefield Publishers, Inc., 2006.

Yenne, Bill. *Great Northern Empire Builder*. St. Paul, MN: MBI Publishing Company, 2005.

Articles

Reddy, John. "Hollywood's Dollar Bills: Pine and Thomas have novel ways of making their Class B movies – among these taking their actors to lunch." *Esquire*, June 1945.

English, Richard. "Gaudiest Producers in Hollywood." *Saturday Evening Post*, Jan. 3, 1953.

Alterman, Eric. "Where's the Rest of Him?" *The Nation*, Mar. 9, 2000.

Pellegrini, Frank. "Reagan at 90: Still a Repository for Our American Dreams." *Time*, Feb. 6, 2001.

"Reagan: The Great Communicator." *BBC News*, Jun. 5, 2004.

Royle, Trevor. "Reagan was the Original Forrest Gump Who Struck Lucky." *The Sunday Herald* (Scotland), Jun. 6, 2004.

Cannon, Lou. "Why Reagan was the 'great communicator.'" *USA Today*, Jun. 6, 2004.

Karnick, S. T. "The Gipper on the Silver Screen." *National Review*, Jun. 8, 2004.

Gibbs, Nancy. "The All-American President: Ronald Wilson Reagan (1911-2004)." *Time*, Jun. 14, 2004.

Klein, Joe. "The Secrets of Reagan's Success." *Time*, Jun. 14, 2004.

Corliss, Richard. "His Days in Hollywood: Ronald Wilson Reagan (1911-2004)." *Time*, Jun. 14, 2004.

Corliss, Richard. "That Old Feeling: Where's the Best of Him?" *Time*, Jun. 16, 2004.

Lane, Anthony. "The Method President." *The New Yorker*, Oct. 18, 2004.

Brookhiser, Richard. "Acting Like a President." *Time*, Apr. 5, 2007.

Hoberman, J. "The Cold War Sci-Fi Parable that Fell to Earth." *New York Times*, Oct. 31, 2008.

"City Set for Premiere." *Springfield News & Leader*, 1 June 1952.

"City Has Big Howdy for Visiting Stars." *Springfield Leader & Press*, 6 June 1952.

"The Stars Arrive." *Springfield Leader & Press*, 6 June 1952.

"Thousands at Premiere of Baseball Film Here." *Springfield Daily News*, 7 June 1952.

"Hillbilly Ronald." *Springfield Leader & Press*, 7 June 1952.

INTERVIEWS

Ralph Nutter, May 23, 2010

Clu Gulager, June 2, 2010

Patricia Neal, June 23, 2010

Russell Johnson, August 16, 2010

Rhonda Fleming, September 14, 2010

Coleen Gray, September 29, 2010

Edwin C. Rice, October 4, 2010

Dorothy Malone, October 7, 2010

Roscoe Black, October 18, 2010

In the early years, Reagan relied on his eyeglasses, but was rarely photographed wearing them. He was one of the first people in the U.S. to adopt contact lenses.
(Author collection)

ABOUT THE AUTHORS

J. HERBERT KLEIN was born in Detroit, Michigan, on August 22, 1921. He joined the U.S. Air Force in 1942 and served in the First Motion Picture Unit, where Captain Ronald W. Reagan was his commanding officer. After his release from the service in 1945, Klein took over the family business – building luxury homes for the rich and famous. In 1956, Klein and colleague Charles Martin produced the film noir classic *Death of a Scoundrel* for Howard Hughes. Subsequently, Klein pioneered talk television, producing programs that appeared on local stations in Los Angeles. In 1964, Klein produced the first American Theatre Awards, a talent competition for college students judged by Hollywood legends such as Robert Wise, director of *West Side Story* and *The Sound of Music*. During the mid-1960s, Klein established a business partnership with Jon Hall, leading man of the 1930s and 1940s, that generated patents and technological innovations. One of the oldest members of the Academy of Motion Picture Arts and Sciences and the Academy of Television Arts and Sciences, Klein is still active in the business as executive producer of International Film Arts – a production company that develops projects for film and television.

MELANIE VILLINES is a critically acclaimed screenwriter, playwright, television writer, novelist, and biographer. Born and raised in Chicago, Melanie lives in Los Angeles.

(Photo of Melanie Villines at The Reagan Library, August 2010, by Jessica Everleth)

Acknowledgments

First and foremost, the authors would like to thank **Nancy Reagan** for allowing us to include excerpts from her husband's love letters in this book and for permission to include the note she wrote to Edwin "Cookie" Rice in 1952. We are also grateful for permission to include several Reagan Family photographs. No words are adequate to express our deep appreciation to Mrs. Reagan for sharing these personal treasures. Thanks, too, to Mrs. Reagan's assistant, **Wren Powell**, for her kind consideration and courtesy regarding our requests.

We extend our gratitude to the late, great **Patricia Neal** for her delightful interview about her friend Ronald Reagan. To our knowledge, this was Ms. Neal's last interview – and in it she expressed her admiration and warm regard for Ronald Reagan. Ms. Neal was a charming, beautiful, generous woman – a unique individual who will never be replaced.

We appreciate **Russell Johnson**'s consideration in granting our interview request. Mr. Johnson is a true gentleman – honest, thoughtful, kind, and humble. A fine actor, great mind, and terrific human being, we thank Mr. Johnson for recalling Hollywood during the early 1950s – both the good times and the "terrible, terrible times."

A big thank you to the beautiful **Rhonda Fleming** for her enthusiasm about discussing her colleague and friend, Ronald Reagan, and the four movies they made together. Ms. Fleming's esteem and admiration for Ronald Reagan was truly inspiring – and her warmth and candor were touching. Thanks, too, to Ms. Fleming's assistant, the delightful **Carla**, for all of her help with our requests and for her keen interest in this project.

We appreciate **Dorothy Malone** speaking with us about her time working with Ronald Reagan on *Law and Order*. She talked about Reagan's charm and upbeat spirit, and how he made the set a fun place to work. Ms. Malone's lovely voice and commanding demeanor reminded us of why she is such a great star. Many thanks, Ms. Malone. Thank you, too, to **Mimi Vanderstraaten** for setting up the interview with her mother – and for sending the wonderful Dorothy Malone/Ronald Reagan photo.

We extend our heartfelt appreciation to **Clu Gulager** who met with us in person to recall his time making *The Killers* (1964) with Ronald Reagan – whose appearance in the movie marked his first and last role as a villain. Mr. Gulager is a charming, inspired gentleman with a terrific sense of humor and incredible recall for details. His insights and anecdotes were amusing, amazing, and among the best we've ever heard anywhere. Thank you, Mr. Gulager.

Thank you to the lovely **Coleen Gray Zeiser** for sharing her reminiscences of working with Ronald Reagan on *Tennessee's Partner*. We were heartened to hear about her admiration for her costar and her warm friendship with both Ronald and Nancy Reagan. Ms. Gray Zeiser's wit and wisdom made the interview a true delight.

Much appreciation goes to Judge **Ralph Nutter**, who generously shared his memories about interacting with the U.S. Air Force First Motion Picture Unit during WWII. Judge Nutter's stories about serving as a combat pilot and flying missions over

Germany and Japan were beyond awe-inspiring. He gave us new insights into the closing months of the war, and how the films shot by the First Motion Picture Unit helped bring about a victory. We are honored that Judge Nutter – a hero, scholar, and all-around great person – spoke with us at length about his experiences.

Our thanks to **Edwin "Cookie" Rice** for sharing his heartwarming story about driving Ronald and Nancy Reagan around Springfield, Missouri, in early June 1952 during a weekend celebration for the premiere of *The Winning Team*. Mr. Rice also generously shared his rare autographed photograph showing his twenty-year-old self driving a future president and his wife, while then-president Harry Truman watched from the parade reviewing stand. We also appreciate Mr. Rice sending a photo of the lovely thank-you note he received from Nancy Reagan. The entire episode is a feel-good, upbeat story – and we're so grateful we could include it in this book. Thanks, too, to Mr. Rice's assistant, **Courtney Smith**, for her consideration in obtaining the photographs.

A huge thank you to **Roscoe Black** for taking time to share his reminiscences about the summer of 1954, when he was twelve years old and the cast and crew from *Cattle Queen of Montana* stayed at his family's St. Mary Lodge near Glacier National Park. Mr. Black's recollections of Ronald Reagan – as a kind, thoughtful, down-to-earth, humble, appreciative, considerate individual – were truly inspiring. The story about his fishing excursion with the film star and future president was an uplifting gem. Mr. Black's remembrances of Reagan make it clear that playing the good guy was not just a role – it was what Reagan was like in real life. Thank you, Mr. Black, for sharing these wonderful stories.

A deep bow goes to **Ned Comstock** of the University of Southern California Cinematic Arts Library. Thank you, Ned, for all the special attention and effort you gave our request – and for going way, way beyond the call of duty. You are a researcher's patron saint – and the USC Cinema Arts Archive is a rich resource with incomparable material. Our profound thanks!

Many thanks to **Sandra Joy Lee Aguilar, Jonathon Auxier,** and **Brett Service** at the Warner Bros. Archives at the University of Southern California's School of Cinematic Arts for your graciousness and outstanding assistance during our numerous visits. It was an honor and a privilege to conduct research at your facility. You are all to be commended for making this wealth of material available to researchers. Thank you and thank you again!

We extend our gratitude to the staff at the Academy of Motion Picture Arts and Sciences **Margaret Herrick Library** for outstanding professionalism, cheerful assistance, and incredible patience. You make doing research a joy and a pleasure – and in such beautiful surroundings. A trip to your facility is cause for elation and almost seems like a vacation. We love that the Margaret Herrick Library staff gets almost as excited as we do when we uncover a significant piece of research material. We really can't say enough good things about you – you are truly wonderful people.

A special thank you to **Lou Cannon**, probably the world's best biographer – and certainly one of the world's best people. Mr. Cannon kindly answered our questions about specific research materials and then shared possible avenues for finding what we were seeking. We feel truly honored by Mr. Cannon's advice and generosity of spirit.

Many others helped us during our journey as we developed this book. Our thanks go to:

Alan K. Rode, writer and film historian, for many valuable insights and much helpful advice.

Brad Olive of the SoCal Nash Club for helping us locate a photo of a 1937 Nash convertible.

Stephon Litwinczuk, film director and producer, for background material about Ronald Reagan.

Dace Taube, Regional History Collection Librarian, Special Collections, Doheny Memorial Library, University of Southern California, for allowing us to use the terrific photos from the USC collection. These photos of buildings really helped set the scene about Reagan's early years in Hollywood. Thanks, too, to **Rachelle Balinas Smith** for her careful attention in fulfilling our requests.

Angela Riggio and **Carol Nishijima**, Charles E. Young Research Library, UCLA, for kindly allowing us to use photos from your remarkable collections.

Valerie Yaros, historian at the Screen Actors Guild, for providing the photo of Reagan when he served as president of the Guild.

Dave Holmgren, historical researcher, for kindly (and reasonably) looking up the articles Reagan wrote for the *Des Moines Register*. It was a pleasure working with someone as efficient, competent, considerate, and honest as you are, Dave.

Jo Ann Donaldson of the *Des Moines Register* for allowing us to use Reagan's 1937 articles in this book. These charming articles offer incredible insights into Reagan's personality, hopes, dreams, and life. Thank you so much for the honor of including these articles, Ms. Donaldson.

Ray Wilson at the Reagan Library, for promptly responding to our frequent queries and for providing the photo of Reagan's model ships. **The Reagan Library** is an incredible resource – and probably one of the most beautiful spots in the world. Everyone should make a visit to this stunning, stimulating location – and climb aboard Air Force One and spend some time in the Oval Office.

Michael Price and the **Springfield-Greene County Library District** for copies of newspaper articles about Reagan's 1952 visit to Springfield, Missouri. Thank you, Michael, for your prompt attention and thoughtful consideration. The articles are remarkable.

Chris Peterson and **Hungry Horse News** in Montana for the wonderful photos of Glacier National Park and Ronald Reagan during the making of *Cattle Queen of Montana*. These beautiful photographs bring the chapter to life. Thank you!

Jerry Murbach at doctormacro.com for the use of his beautiful scans. You are a kind, generous soul, Jerry – and we greatly appreciate your wonderful consideration.

Pete Soule for graciously answering our questions about model shipbuilding and generously providing a rare photo of Reginald Denny's Hobby Shop in Hollywood. Thank you so much, Pete!

West Peterson of the Antique Automobile Club of America for providing a photo of a 1938 LaSalle and helping us identify the model and year of Reagan's LaSalle in the photo included in Chapter 11. Thank you for your courtesy, West!

Chuck Anderson for forwarding the stunning photo of Rodd Redwing from the Ken Jones Collection. Your kindness is most appreciated, Chuck.

First Motion Picture Unit vets **Stanley Frazen** and **Gene Marks** for carefully (and kindly!) reading the manuscript, pointing out errors, and offering suggestions. You are two reasons why the Allies won WWII!

A huge thank you to **Margaret Werner,** who listened to the story from the beginning and offered suggestions and insights based on her vast knowledge of movies, actors, and Hollywood. Margaret, we appreciate your reading, proofing, and editing multiple versions of the book. If it weren't for you, Zachary Scott would have turned up as Zachary Taylor at one point. Thank you for catching all of our mistakes and helping us realize where and when we needed to make revisions. Your brilliant mind, sweeping knowledge, and deep wisdom are an inspiration to everyone who knows you. Our bottomless appreciation!

Jessica Everleth and **Hunter Villines** for the trip to the Reagan Library – and to Jessica for the author's photo and ongoing support and insights.

Mike Everleth for assistance with the photo files and a myriad of additional details. You are always ready to lend a hand, and we truly appreciate it!

Mary Jo Degens, number one Reagan fan and trusted friend, for ongoing interest in this project and helpful advice about the Reagan Library.

Julie Johnson for continual support, insight, encouragement – and overall brilliance. Thank you, Julie!

Connie Scanlon of Bogfire for her beautiful, inspired design of this book. Thank you, Connie, for making these pages sing!

Cary Klein for belief in this project and unwavering support and enthusiasm.

And, finally, much gratitude to the man who inspired this book. People who knew **Ronald Reagan** considered him a kind, considerate, thoughtful, humble man. Hollywood never went to his head, and he never went Hollywood. Throughout his career, Reagan remained the same good-natured, courteous, affable, optimistic, self-effacing person he'd been from the start. He managed to succeed in Hollywood – and far beyond – despite all these admirable qualities. Sometimes good guys do finish first.

Code of the Secret Service, 1939.
(Author collection)

FROM 1981-1988, RONALD REAGAN SERVED AS PRESIDENT OF THE UNITED STATES.

(Photo: Reagan Library)

The Ronald Reagan Trail traverses small towns in Northwestern Illinois – such as Tampico, Dixon, and Galesburg – where Reagan grew up.

In 1974, the Reagans purchase Rancho Del Cielo – located in the Santa Ynez Mountains north of Santa Barbara, California. During and after his presidency, Reagan hosts many dignitaries – including Margaret Thatcher, Queen Elizabeth II, and Mikhail Gorbachev – on the property, dubbed the Western White House.

www.ingramcontent.com/pod-product-compliance
Lightning Source LLC
Chambersburg PA
CBHW061634040426
42446CB00010B/1410